MW00436107

TWO RACES BEYOND THE ALTAR

TWO RACES BEYOND THE ALTAR

By
PATRICK HUBER

Boston
BRANDEN PRESS
Publishers

© Copyright, 1976, by Branden Press, Inc.
Library of Congress Catalog Card Number 75-30268
ISBN 0-8283-1646-5
Printed in the United States of America

Among the many people who have contributed to this book, Thomas Papino of the University of Miami has been particularly vital because of his help in editing and rewriting the manuscript. Emotional as well as editorial support also was provided by Martha Kennedy of the *Cincinatti Post*. Other Miamians to whom I am indebted include David Berni, Thomas Healey Jr., Robert James, Jo Ann McGeorge, Hal Metcalf, Roberta Papino, Agustin Recio, Isis Recio, Joan Timmons, and Nancy Young.

To Mother,
whose cautious nature making her wonder about the desirability
of her son's plan to marry a black woman, was dramatically overshadowed by an openmindedness and warmth that enabled her to
be a major asset to that marriage.

CONTENTS

INTRODUCTION

It was pleasant riding on the bus — more pleasant than usual. My bus connections were good to and from work compared to those of most people in Miami, thanks to this City of Coral Gables Route running near our house every thirty minutes. The Coral Gables passengers had been left off near their $90,000 homes, and now in the last ten minutes of the ride it was just us ordinary working people. Most of them were more friendly than the riders on big city buses, and a lot of us had gotten to recognize each other. In fact, earlier that week when I'd fallen asleep, the regular rider sitting behind me had awakened me so I'd not ride past my stop. I was definitely awake today, however, looking forward to getting home.

It was typical February weather, typical for Miami that is, which for us natives of the middlewest meant it was actually good solid September weather transplanted to February. This was the time of year I liked in Miami, the only time when it was cool enough to feel any vigor in life. I looked at the tan knit slacks I had on — those new ones I felt were more than my job deserved. They weren't anything extravagant, but better than the three-year-old ones I usually wore. My mother had said when she had given them to me for Christmas that I should not follow my usual practice of letting them sit around until they were out of style. Of course it seems funny that the son of a third-generation retail clothier should have to be persuaded to wear a decent looking pair of slacks; but then there were a number of things about me that weren't quite typical for the son of a small but well-established clothing store owner in a friendly little Iowa town of 1200 people.

In any event, the pants made me feel good. So did remembering about kissing my wife and six-year-old good-by that morning, something I did with almost as much deliberation as deciding to wear a new pair of slacks. In fact, I had not kissed my wife several times two weeks earlier because we had argued after she suggested that we see a marriage counselor. I had said we could solve our own problems. She hadn't said any more about it; and I was glad she agreed with me. Tonight I could kiss her — as I had the night before — knowing it was not something automatic, but a reflection of true love.

By now we were two minutes from the stop, and I was looking forward to our eating supper together and then spending some time together. Since it was Friday, there was no school or work for anybody to worry about the next day, so we could slow down from our weekday pace.

On my block-and-a-half walk from the bus stop, my spirits were raised even a bit higher as I was greeted by Dallas Berger, our neighbor of some four houses away. Dallas is a great guy, and speaking to him is always a little boost. We didn't usually run into any of our neighbors — why we weren't always sure — so speaking to any neighbor was a delight.

As I approached the house, I realized my wife might be late getting home from work, since the car was not in the carport. More likely, since it was Friday, she was probably grocery shopping for the weekend.

Walking in the front door, I went through the living room, glanced at the pile of groceries on the kitchen table, and walked to the bathroom. "My daughter may have a piano lesson tonight, and may be on her way there now," I said to myself while in the bathroom.

As I went to the kitchen, I decided I'd better start putting away some of the groceries since they were all over the floor as well as on the table; and my wife might be bringing in some more in a few minutes. I started, and stopped!

By the first sack I saw it. The note — the type others get, but not me.

"Dear Pat," I read, still believing this note was to tell me whether or not to start supper before they returned. "Meat is in

10

crock pot. Everything else in refrigerator. String beans & pork & beans. All food in refrigerator you know how to cook. Look through it. This is best I could organize. I told you I would take the alternative of leaving. So we have."

Then I knew, but I could not believe. Certainly I had said if she didn't like the way things were at our house, she could leave; but certainly she knew I didn't mean it literally. She understood me; I understood her — I thought.

I did what I suppose most spouses do when nine years of seemingly happy marriage suddenly collapses. I asked questions — questions about our married life, particularly about those things which distinguished it from others.

CHAPTER I

One Night and Nine Years

The line was dead as I hung up the receiver. I might as well have been.

"You don't think I have any ability. I don't think you respect me for anything," the voice at the other end of the line had just charged.

"Well — ah — well I can see why you have been angered at me recently for a few things, but let's not forget all those good times — those eight or nine years, actually those eleven years," I responded. "You know I respected you then."

"I don't know! I don't think you ever respected me."

That really hit hard. We had agreed that everything had not been just right in the last year; but wasn't everything fine up until then? We hadn't covered up a problem for those nine years, had we? Or had we?

"I must have respected you or I wouldn't have married you in the first place," came the reply. "Why else would I have married you?"

"I think you married me so you could save me from the slums. You gave yourself credit for that just last month," she said with increased emotion. "And, *if you respected me,* you would not have called me nigger."

The phone hung up.

The pile of white flesh that hung up the receiver thirty seconds later was upset — upset because I knew she was partly wrong, and more upset because I knew she was partly right. Besides, I was amazed — amazed it had taken us almost a decade to uncover complexities of a biracial marriage, complexities we had just assumed never existed.

Stumbling from the phone to the television set to turn on Walter Cronkite, I thought. As the first story came on, I thought about the seemingly stable future facing me as a young newspaperman eleven years earlier. I was a white middle-class graduate of the best graduate school of journalism in the country — Columbia University, class of '63 — courting a black gal from a place called Bedford Stuyvesant — which is anything but middle class.

I was ready to bring the truth to the world as a hardworking, investigative reporter heralding the needs of the poor and the downtrodden. Now my hopes were gone, my newspaper career was ended, and the wife whom I had married as the "disadvantaged one" was now making more money and getting more attention and credit than I ever got.

I shut off Cronkite a few moments later and walked back to the living room. As the TV flickered out, I remembered the appearance Silvia and I had been asked to make just two years earlier on a Miami TV station to discuss interracial marriage. Silvia, that's her name, and I had always delighted in telling everybody that in our case, the biracial aspect of our marriage had rarely hurt and frequently helped it. The Friday night before Saturday's taping of the show, we agreed to say basically the following:

It is a mistake to conclude the difference between a black spouse and a white spouse is a superficial one of skin color rather than a deep-seated difference. The bigger mistake is to assume that a significant difference between the couples is automatically a handicap. There are differences between all couples — including those resulting from their being of the opposite sex. The differences between some couples are relatively small, and this may help some couples and hurt others. Likewise, with couples whose differences are great. In our case, we have used our differences for the benefit of each of us.

At 9:00 A.M. Saturday morning, we got a call telling us that the program had been cancelled. During the next two years we got indications that our thinking might not have told the whole story.

Sitting in the living room beside the one floor lamp Silvia had left in the house, I opened up the textbook for the statistics course I was taking at the University of Miami — taking at minimal cost thanks to the fact Silvia worked there. As I started to study, I concentrated less on ratios, means, and probability than

13

on jealousy, my jealousy that she had said on the phone she was getting A's in the two graduate-level courses she was taking. An A was not the question in this undergraduate statistics course, the question was whether I would pass. I had been explaining my B's and C's compared to Silvia's A's during the last year by saying the education courses she took were easy while my accounting courses were tough. As I turned the page, not knowing what I'd read, I again heard her stating: "You don't give me credit for anything. When I get an A, it seems as if you're always remembering that my undergraduate grades were below average while yours were above average.

It's strange. I realized she had worked fulltime while in college, while I had not worked at all. Indeed I had been impressed from the beginning with her ambition to get a degree in spite of the odds, and I had always been proud of her for that, assuming she realized that I was a little bit smarter than she. By now she had had enough of that assumption.

At this time the peas were burning, so I went into the kitchen to take a look. Meals of husbands without wives are not usually known for their culinary brilliance. But here a little more was involved. As I ate the junk that had come out of the cans, I contrasted it to the meals Silvia had served recently. Hers weren't the best, but better than this. After using better judgement for seven or eight years, I had started comparing her cooking with my mother's cooking. Although not the first husband to make this mistake, I had caused more tension than the typical husband comparing wife to mom because my mom was not black, not Spanish, and not a professional woman.

The table was in direct line with the carport. This didn't make the meal any more digestible. Of course there wasn't any car there: she had it, and that is not uncommon in any separation. What was uncommon was that only one of us had a driver's license, my having been denied one because of my diabetic condition. That was just a quirk of fate and nothing to get bothered about. What *was* hard to swallow was to see how the tables had turned. Here I was without a car or license, handicapped in employment and otherwise because of my dependence on public transportation, while the woman I had courted at the end of the subway stop could now speed around town at will.

Eleven years earlier it had been I with the car — paid for in cash — and the driver's license, dating a twenty-three-year-old who had never driven, never owned a car, and did not have a relative who owned one. I remembered the first time I drove my used car to pick Silvia up for a date. She had to explain to me that the reason two of her nephews came running to us moments after I parked was because rarely did they know someone who *knew* someone who owned a car; and they wanted to take advantage of the occasion by looking it over closely.

As I stared at the carport, my irrationality had not become so great as to make me think access to auto transportation is a basic ingredient in marital relationships. But I began to wonder if this auto business might tell a little bit about ourselves.

The driving situation seemed normal at the beginning. It was wife's idea to learn to drive and husband was not overly excited; but that is normal enough. Wife suggested a driving instructor, and husband said there was no need to spend that extra money, since he was a good driver. It was normal enough for her to be frightened on the first on-the-road lesson as she zoomed down a rural New Jersey road at five miles an hour. And then running off the road and through thirty feet of ditch, well maybe that wasn't quite the usual thing to do.

But the ditch business was certainly nothing of great importance, particularly when the landlord was very cooperative in helping replace the three large rocks she had plowed away from his stone fence. We jokingly agreed immediately thereafter that a professional instructor was well worth the money. Soon she was a good driver and had a license, and mine had been taken away by the state of New York.

It had bothered me that throughout almost our entire married life, I had been dependent on Silvia for auto transportation. Was my concern increased because she was black? I think not — not for most of the time, anyway. In the last year or two, however, she had become increasingly independent; and her role in our family had become dominant, making me less secure. The tables had turned: I had dropped from master to servant in many ways.

15

As long as I was a driver-turned-passenger, that was a problem unrelated to race. But now my having dropped from driver to passenger was placed alongside other events, as part of a chain of events converting the master into servant. Because the driving matter had become part of this chain, this "automotive servitude," like all other instances of "servitude," was made more difficult to bear because the new master was black.

Then there was the value of the car. I had gotten it in my Iowa hometown in 1971 while working for my mother there. At the time none of us expressed any concern about her paying for some of it: my mother wasn't hurting financially, and she was voluntarily giving something to her only living descendant. The car wasn't just mine, of course: it belonged to Silvia, too; and nobody thought anything of that. In fact, we decided to have it registered in her name, since she was the driver in the family.

Now as I stared toward the carport, my view was blocked by a piece of paper lying on the table, a piece of paper titled "Silvia Huber vs. Patrick Huber," demanding that in settlement of divorce of said partner, Mrs. Huber was to become the sole owner of that car, as well as the house in which I was sitting, and one-half of whatever else we owned.

"It would be bad enough," my thought burned inside, "if I had to give up a car that belonged to the two of us, but it is infuriating to give up a car that she didn't even own half of, or at least buy half of." Of course we had said at the wedding altar, "What is mine is yours and what is yours is mine," and I had said it sincerely. Perhaps it had taken a divorce suit to make me realize I did not mean it literally. My pre-marriage bank account, the free clothing and money from my family were for the two of us equally — except, of course, I was always to be in charge of it. Today I not only could no longer be her financial master, I felt like her victim.

I remembered that just after buying that car her boss had told me that he liked the stripes — which happened to be black — on our otherwise all-white 1972 Duster. I joked: "There's a place for the black as long as the place is right and the white is up on top." His black face smiled broadly at my

16

joke. Now I wondered if maybe it was more than a joke.

As I stared at the divorce petition, I read it again, since I had only read it ten or twelve times since bringing it home that afternoon. I tried to console myself with the thought that probably no husband likes to find out that his estranged wife is demanding sole possession of the house in which they have been living. Certainly I was not the only man who put up his life's savings to purchase a house, while his wife purchased none of it, so to speak. That's not a matter of color, that is just a have marrying a have-not. Race did not complicate this economic frustration, except for that business about it being a little more difficult to switch from master to servant when the new master is black.

There was a bright spot in the divorce petition. Maybe. Although it said our marriage was irreconcilable, it then got a little bit contradictory and said, "Silvia Huber prays that she and her husband will see a marriage counselor in an effort to resolve their differences." This sounded a little bit hopeful. I had been disgusted a month earlier when she suggested counseling, but now I was glad she was still willing to consider it.

Our disagreement about using counseling resulted from a basic difference in our backgrounds. Not a difference of race or religion, but one which involves a much greater sense of tribalistic loyalty. The difference: she was a sociology major, and I a political science major. I had told her that sociologists, particularly those who had taken as many psychology courses as she, sometimes tended to overestimate the value of counseling. She came the closest to getting me to go to a counselor when she said they are needed to provide a neutral sounding board for a couple just as the United Nations is needed to provide a diplomatic link between hostile countries. I was impressed, but not sold.

Now, as I thumbed through the petition again, I wished that even though I disagreed that we needed to see a counselor, I had agreed to see one. That is what I had done February 3, but that was only because she had already gone ahead with the divorce suit and had left home two days earlier, leaving me no alternative.

Anyway, it was now February 13, the divorce petition was in my hand, and the afternoon had been emotion-packed. It sounds like a soap box opera to write that one Pat Huber, unaware about its being his wedding anniversary, arranged to pick up his divorce petition after work on February 13, 1974, and then became sentimental about it on his way home from the courthouse. It sounds melodramatic, but that happened to be the way it happened on this particular day.

Soon after getting to work that morning at Aristar, Inc., a nationwide conglomerate, I went into the office of Tom Healey to borrow his telephone. Tom was a financial analyst there and I was only an anonymous member of the accounting department; but he did not let his higher status interfere with our good friendship. Since he knew what the reason was for my call, he asked if he should leave. I said please don't bother, and proceded to call the Dade County Courthouse to find out when, where and how I would be served with that unwanted petition. I arranged to pick it up that afternoon and asked Tom if he'd take me over after work. He agreed without hesitancy, although he reminded me that at that time of day it was faster to walk than ride to the courthouse. He repeated himself as we crawled along Brickell Avenue that afternoon.

"I can believe that," I responded, "but I guess the main reason I asked you to go along is because not only are you my closest friend, but your stability and your experience in military security are what I need at a time like this."

"Don't kid yourself," he said quickly. "If I were in your shoes right now, I'd be scared to death. I'd be worrying about child support and a lot of things."

"At least that's one thing I don't have to worry about, since she makes more money than I do. At least I don't think so, but maybe I should be worrying," I admitted to him.

At the courthouse everything was routine, at least until I started reading the petition through the second line, where it said that Silvia Silva and Don Patrick Huber were married in Brooklyn, New York, on February 13, 1965.

I'm not the sentimental type. In fact, Silvia had wished I were a little more that way and I had wished she were a little

18

less that way. We used to jokingly attribute the difference to her Spanish and my German ancestry. Lately we hadn't been joking. When we opposed each other's emotionalism or lack of it, we assumed we were opposing the background to which we attributed it.

Once the suit had been filed, she seemed to be the Prussian and I the emotional Spaniard. I could not read "February 13, 1965", without thinking how different things looked on February 13, 1974. As I read the petition out loud after we got back into the car, Tom said in his thoughtful, restrained way: "I think she really is going to go through with the divorce, Pat, even though I've told you that might not be the case. I think you had better get a lawyer."

Usually when I rode home with Tom, he dropped me off at the bus station near his apartment. That night he gave me a ride all the way home. I needed it. When he left me off, I was still thinking about February 13, 1965. It had been wonderful. I hadn't been emotional about it, although I tolerated her slight emotionalism as an inevitable weakness of females, Puerto Ricans, and slum dwellers. I had admitted lately that I wished I had spent $50 to have pictures taken of that joyous occasion rather than prove I was one-fourth Scotch by saying we should not spend money on something as unproductive as wedding pictures. In fact, after supper that night in 1974, I looked at the small photo on the bookcase taken of Silvia and me six months earlier. Each of us liked the picture. It almost served as a wedding picture. She was just as attractive, even though her busy days since coming to Miami could be detected on her face, and her waist would not slide into her twenty-two inch wedding dress. Her Afro was a sharp contrast to the straightened hair she wore up until 1971; but it now was just as much a part of her as the growing black consciousness that inspired it.

As for me, there was a wrinkle or two on the forehead now, but my only other physical difference couldn't be noticed — the fact I couldn't part my hair the way I used to, thanks to our adventures in Louisville, Kentucky, some seven years earlier. In the very pleasant neighborhood near the University of Cincinnati where we once lived, however, as well as in that ghetto

19

in Brooklyn where so much happened, and in that peaceful little community of Newark, Ohio, people would have no trouble recognizing us. In fact, we had agreed not very long ago that we should start making plans to visit some of our widely-distributed friends.

Pictures make one dream; dirty dishes don't. I, the one who ten and eleven years ago had told Silvia I was much neater than the average bachelor, had left two-days'-worth of dishes in the sink.

It was hard not to notice the dishes as I turned away from the picture back in the direction of the kitchen. The dishes did remind me that during our courtship I had told Silvia forcefully I was not looking for the typical housewife whose prime goal in life was to bake good bread and raise ten children. I felt she was going too far, however, when she started demanding a couple years ago that we get a maid to do some housework. For several months I thought, and then finally told her that she had lost all sense of economic reality, that we could not afford that and there was no need for it. That has been said by many husbands. What has not been said by many is this: "Silvia, you must be trying to compete with those nouveau riche blacks who think they must prove their financial success by hiring someone to do those service jobs usually performed by blacks working for whites."

That turned the whole maid issue into one of human dignity. That my comment might have been true with a few couples and not true with most is beside the point. So was the lack of tact in making it. The crucial factor was that such an exchange was possible only because the marriage was biracial. The biracialness of the marriage had permitted what started as a mere matter of economics to become converted into a damaging emotional issue.

As I turned toward the living room, deciding to put off the dishes until tomorrow, I realized this is the very same thing I had been accusing her of doing for months. Whenever her plans to do the dishes were delayed, I told her they were no less work tomorrow than today. Here was an aspect of the dirty-dish matter unrelated to philosophy, race, religion, sex or politics: it was merely a product of its being easier to give logical advice to

20

others than for one to act logically himself.

As I finally plunged my hands beneath the surface of the dishwater, the eight or ten cans of food on the counter reminded me of the thirty or forty such cans she had left the day she departed, along with a wide variety of other food. This doesn't sound quite like the typical divorce tale, particularly when you consider the good supper she had left me cooking in the crock pot that February 1.

"But if she was really concerned about me, why did she leave in the first place?" I asked myself. "Or at least why didn't she drop the divorce suit so I wouldn't have to pay for a lawyer? As I told her over the phone a little earlier, I could eat a lot of restaurant meals for what the lawyer would cost."

If she did not drop the suit within twenty or thirty days, I would have to respond to it in order to keep her from getting everything. I told her over the phone this meant my hiring a lawyer to answer her suit unless she dropped it. I explained she could always reinstitute the suit if she wanted to, so wouldn't be disarming herself if she stopped and let us try to resolve our differences.

"I have already paid for the suit. It cost me a lot of money," she said curtly. "Whether or not you want to hire a lawyer is your decision. I am done making your decisions for you."

This told little about our marriage or our divorce, except it proved that she no longer trusted me. Indeed, she had indicated she feared me physically, financially, and legally because she felt I was stronger in all those ways. Many divorces involve similar sentiments; and indeed many married women have such feelings. A sentiment that seemed different in Silvia's case was the desire to be independent.

As I finished the dishes, I remembered her once saying to me that she was a much more independent person than her quiet manner probably ever indicated to me. This independent nature had been brought out in her work as Assistant Director of Affirmative Action at the University of Miami, a position which demanded she be directly involved in obtaining increased rights and opportunities for women and members of minority groups, particularly blacks. I thought of this during our phone

21

conversation that night, when she told me she was going to a conference — one scheduled for the following week — and wanted to know if I would take care of our daughter. Actually she asked if I "wanted" to take care of our daughter, adding: "If you don't want to, I can arrange something easily enough."

About half the conferences she attended involved woman's rights, and the other half minority rights. She went only three or four times a year, but we had been equally enthusiastic about them when she first started attending. We both generally agreed on their purpose and thought them professionally beneficial to her. After she returned from them, she would summarize them for me and we would discuss the ideas expressed. After seven or eight of them, I began joking with her boss and her that when she went to a conference on female rights, she came back thinking all men are bad, and when she attended a minority rights conference, she came home with the idea all whites are bad. "Either way, I lose," I joked to him.

Now the joke was over. I was convinced enough that such activities strained our relationship that I had considered the previous week asking her boss if he would discourage her from attending such conferences for a few months until we had had a chance to work out our family differences. I gave up the idea from lack of influence, not because the idea seemed any less sound.

The impact of either type conference was similar, but there seemed to be more problems when I was the "wrong" sex than when the "wrong" color. As luck would have it, this conference regarded women's rights, and so I surmised that whatever progress we made in rebuilding our marriage by the following Wednesday would be more than neutralized by the conference. Later developments seemed to confirm this suspicion.

After finally completing that "feminine chore" called dishwashing, I wandered into the living room and slouched down on a well-stuffed cane chair, one of the set we bought secondhand in New Jersey in 1965 for a total of $90. Nine years, five moves and about 3500 miles later, the stuff looked lousy. Silvia had been telling me this for at least a year. But I had been raised in

22

the rural midwest where simplicity and frugality were virtues. In recent years I had tried to become even tighter in order to compensate for a limited income.

The differences between Silvia's and my race and economic background erected a wall between Silvia and me as far as home furnishings were concerned. First of all, she had never known closely anyone rich or poor who worshipped frugality, so she saw little logic in it. What well-to-do people she had known, particularly before marriage, were all urban, predominantly Jewish, and had money because of their earning power. In my hometown, those who were well-to-do got that way by saving a lot, not because they earned so much. This difference appeared when Silvia wrote to me in 1973 at a Catholic marriage encounter weekend:

I don't feel the importance or urgency of money as you do. I feel that if accumulating money is so important, then you need to read more on ways of getting rich.

Often when I told Silvia that the only true frugality was that practiced in rural America, she replied by pointing out my mother's furniture was much better than ours, overlooking the fact my mother happened to be a little older than we were.

Another problem was that Silvia's Miami friends, many of whom were black, spent money like typical U.S. middle class couples in their thirties: they spent more than they had. I told her that we did not want to behave like financially irresponsible people who did not know how to handle money because they had never had it before. Often I was thinking about the finances of black friends, often I spoke about the finances of black friends, and often we ended up debating about race rather than talking about finances. I reminded her more than was necessary of the black couple we knew who bought $4000 worth of furniture on credit upon getting married, and ended up six months later with a divorce and furniture for which neither could pay.

Our different economic backgrounds were even more important than our racial differences when it came to the subject of the family budget. Take the set of furniture in the living room where I was now sitting. I said any sofa that didn't fall apart was good enough for me as long as we did not have a dossier full of stocks and did not give extensively to help the world's less fortunate. Wanting to be charitable, I forgot that it is easier to proclaim a habitat of monastic simplicity if you have already enjoyed material comforts for thirty years. Perhaps this is why I didn't hear Silvia clearly when she said it was time we settle down and have a modest but respectable house. I compared her pre-marriage housing to her post-marriage housing and thought she must consider herself living in splendor; she compared our housing at age thirty with that of my parents at age fifty-five and thought she was being shortchanged.

I had opened a little earlier that evening an invitation addressed to Silvia and me for the house opening of Silvia's boss, an abode in the $60,000-plus class in southwest Miami. I had not seen the house, neither had Silvia, but she had talked about it. I couldn't really tell if she was desirous of such a place, or merely talking about it as interesting news — or what. I thought about that walk which had started out in Central Park in 1964 on a very pleasant summer evening — the walk which ended in Times Square one and one-half hours and one marriage proposal later, but included a lot of money talk up around 80th Street. We talked there about our economic needs and desires, and seemed to understand each other. Had I changed? Had she changed? Had we both changed — or what?

My opposition to keeping up with the Joneses had gotten so strong in Miami that I hesitated to have Heather, our daughter, take piano lessons as early as age four, because I feared that Silvia's goal was only to get our little girl "introduced to culture" at an earlier age than anyone else's youngster. As I walked into Heather's bedroom that night, I noticed that the $150 piano we had gotten her for Christmas, 1972, was now gone. Silvia and her Puerto Rican friend had moved out everything else she wanted the day she left, but the piano had been a little heavy. I had hoped the piano had stayed because Silvia was planning to be gone only a short while. It was not until she hired somebody to move it that I really took her seriously about this divorce business. But now I had learned that she was very serious.

She had told me a week or so ago she had been more serious about a lot of things through the years than I realized. Maybe I

24

had overlooked some of her serious statements because although I was tolerant of blacks, I could not believe them to be quite as serious as most whites. The big stereotype involved here, however, was not racial but sexual: although I was tolerant of women, I could not believe them to be quite as serious as men. I was more pro-women's-rights than most men, but was not among that very small minority that took them just as seriously as they did men.

Unfortunately, it took something this dramatic to show me just how serious women can be. I thought during that February, and still think, that female and black stereotypes worked in reverse on Silvia. Although definitely a determined and responsible person who carried out what she said she was going to do, she felt particularly obligated to stick to her word because she was a woman. She often spoke critically of women when they fit into the stereotype of being indecisive or undependable. Silvia was out to prove that she was not the woman who could not make up her mind. Maybe she was out also to prove that she was not the black who couldn't make up his mind or had no well-defined plan of future action.

Naturally Heather's closets were empty, as were Silvia's. This was no news. It was a reminder, though, that Silvia meant what she said and was not coming back — at least for a long while. Besides, the missing dresses included four or five that had come free of charge from Huber's Clothing Store, Clarksville, Iowa: that made me stop and think, and then admit to myself, as I had with the car, that although such things were for the two of us, they were really my long-term loans to her. They were gifts, but I had always wanted the gift tag kept on them.

I decided that before going to bed, I would get a few minutes relaxation and diversion by reading the newspaper. I read for fifteen or twenty minutes, limiting most of my readership to the front page and sports section — something an ex-newspaperman should never admit to doing. The Watergate controversy still seemed important; but I started thinking more about 1963, my apartment in New Jersey, and *The New York Times*.

Several months before Silvia and I got married — I couldn't remember that this event took place in October, 1963 — the

25

Times ran a front page story about interracial marriage, documenting that it was on the increase and discussing the implications of it. Both of us read it closely and were boosted a little by learning about others who had taken the same marital adventure we were planning to take. There had only been one comment in that story that had bothered me, a statement that an interracial marriage involved a "sick" relationship. Of course we both knew better at the time and sympathized with the Ph.D. who was stupid enough to make such a remark; but now I wondered if maybe he knew a little bit about that of which he spoke.

If I had been able to find where we kept the Oct. 18, 1963 issue of the *Times*, I would have learned that the man quoted was Dr. Nathan W. Ackerman, a clinical professor of psychiatry at Columbia University. He stated: "It is abnormal in this time and place to have an interracial experience. In this particular transitional stage of our culture here in America, this is a relatively abnormal thing to do."

Well, I wasn't sick — I didn't think. I would agree more, as did Silvia, with most of the authorities quoted in the story who said a biracial marriage had problems not existent in others, but had some advantages too. I knew that divorce suit was not setting on the living room table because my wife and I were different colors; but it was impossible to avoid asking if maybe a biracial marriage involved more friction than had been openly revealed in our nine years of apparently genuine harmony.

So much for the questions. It was past bedtime, and I had to make sure and catch the bus in the morning — because Silvia would not be there to give me a ride if I missed it. So off through the barren living room, past Heather's empty bedroom, past Silvia's empty closet, and into bed, the emptiest thing of all. Empty closet, empty house, empty wallet, empty refrigerator, empty bed.

CHAPTER II

Wedding Day

Her smile, always photogenic, was larger and more genuine than ever.

"I felt so good about it. I was even nervous. Weren't you? " Silvia asked. "You didn't sound nervous at all."

"I was determined not to get excited about the ceremony, but became excited anyway," I answered. "I'd have to admit I felt good all over."

We were at the doorway. I put my arms around her, saying I would break my usual policy of not kissing in public. "Only once or twice, though," I warned. She smiled after the two kisses, telling me without words that she liked the way I limited my emotions in order to deepen our love, not to limit it.

She had a little rice on her dress, but not very much for a bride of four minutes. We didn't need rice to know we were married. We didn't need many of the usual "wedding necessities." There was no photographer: I had thought picture-taking would be a waste of money. No flowers on the altar. The bride and bridesmaids and mothers had corsages — total cost $30 — but Silvia hadn't worried about matching them with the dresses. She and I blended well and that was what counted.

The service had become particularly meaningful when Father Sullivan told the congregation: "Two people here today have chosen to be united in marriage and live their lives as one." We were warmed because we knew him and we knew each other. Although the words were common, we knew we had indeed chosen each other. The union had not been prescribed or even encouraged by our families or by society: we were marrying because we had chosen to marry. Father Sullivan also knew we

27

had chosen each other, because he had spent several hours skill-fully examining with us our reasons for wanting to marry each other. Thus louder than any emotional outbursts or traditional horn honking was his closing prayer: "May you be joined and love each other and your Lord."

He greeted us as we stood at the doorway. The doors be-longed to St. James Church in Brooklyn Heights. It was on the dividing line between the wealth of Brooklyn Heights and the low-income housing projects in Fort Greene. Father Sullivan had been assigned there recently to provide a Spanish-speaking priest to serve Puerto Ricans — such as Silvia's sister, Benedicta — in Fort Greene. Benedicta had recommended him to Silvia after Silvia had tried elsewhere. Here's how Silvia described her efforts to get us married in another church:

I belonged to a girls' group in a Spanish church in the Williamsburg section of Brooklyn from 1959 through 1964. I attended the group regularly and hardly ever missed its monthly Communion. When a member of the group got married, the rest of us would participate in the ceremony and this was very meaningful to us. When I went to the priest and told him I would like to be married in the church, he was bothered about Pat's color and religion. He said statistics showed our marriage was not likely to succeed and he did not approve of it. He asked if my fiance would become Catholic and I told him no. He then said I could not go up to the altar to get married. I could accept this, but then he said the girls' group could not parti-cipate. That made me mad! He then indicated he did not want to marry us at all. With Father Sullivan, it was a matter of his respecting the religious convictions of both Pat and me.

Thanks to Father Sullivan, here we were at the doorway. The date was February 13, 1965, because we agreed we should not marry until she finished her undergraduate work at Brooklyn College, and that had been done just twelve days earlier.

It was 4:45 P.M. The 4:00 P.M. ceremony had started about ten minutes late. Silvia, who always was on time, was late. Pat, who never was on time, had been a little less late. The first couple to arrive had almost left before the action started. Jon Amsel, Grinnell College roommate and fellow graduate, class of '62, and the son of a successful Ridgefield, Connecticut lum-berman, was not quite sure he and his wife had come to the right place for Pat Huber's wedding. Here is how he described it later:

After we had been in Brooklyn a little while, I began to look at the map and invitation to make sure we were going to the right place. Once we got to the address we were still sure we were lost, but since the church name matched the invitation, we decided to go inside. I asked somebody if Pat Huber was getting married there, and he couldn't speak English. I not only didn't see you, I didn't see very many people your color. I wasn't sure we were in the right place until I saw Dan Figgins.

Dan Figgins, also Grinnell Class of '62, was best man. We had much in common: native Iowans, middle-road Protestants, idealists, non-smokers, teetotalers, and very limited users of profanity. He was a much better best man than this man deserved. On paper he looked good: Phi Betta Kappa, Ivy League Ph.D. candidate, member of United States delegation to the United Nations. More importantly, he had a humility and sensitivity for the needs of others.

By coincidence, my selections for wedding participants represented a diversity of religions. Alongside Methodist Figgins, the two ushers were a Jew and a Catholic, Reuven Rosenfelder and Tom McDevitt, two newspapermen with whom I lived during my bachelor days in New Jersey.

Silvia's wedding personnel was headed by her sister, Benedicta, the maid of honor. The bride's one older sister came to New York City as a teenager one and one-half years after their divorced mother took Silvia there in 1949. The two girls had always been very close, working with their mother to meet the challenges of a family without a male member, faced with the problems of living in a culture foreign to their own. Walking down the same isle as Benedicta was her eight-year-old daughter, Sandra, who served as flower girl. Watching were her two sons and her husband of twelve years, Delores Nieves, who worked on a production line in a Long Island plastics plant.

The Nieves family lived in nearby Fort Greene at Forty-five Fleet Walk, a picturesque name for a very un-picturesque street in a low-income project. Silvia had gotten to know Daria Brown, one of the bridesmaids, because she had lived next door to Benedicta. Daria's mother, a practical nurse, had become friends with Benedicta and sometimes advised her about rearing her children.

While Daria was black, the other bridesmaid, Priscilla, was Puerto Rican. In fact, she had been a neighbor in Santurce, Puerto Rico, who by chance happened to refind Silvia among New York City's seven million people. Silvia retells the story:

Priscilla was our backdoor neighbor up until we left Puerto Rico in 1949. Six years later, my mother (Cecilia) recognized Priscilla's sister at a factory in the garment

29

district where they were both working. I soon re-met Priscilla and we became friends again. Her father had died when we were both six years old. I can remember the year because of the good time we both had at the funeral. That's a terrible thing to say, but it's the truth. At that time in Puerto Rico, the bodies were kept at the home. Spanish Catholics conducted a nine-day wake and people would be coming in all day and night to say rosaries. Priscilla and I and all the other kids our age got to stay up until 10:00 or 11:00 P.M. That was very late for us and we got to hear a lot of gossip... We had a ball.

Here we had participated not in a funeral service but in a wedding service. We were standing at the doorway. Near it was Cecilia, Silvia's mother; and I had already hesitated too long to introduce her to my family. Cecilia's English was bad and she was overly conscious about it. My mother had never spoken to someone of Spanish background, but she was more self-conscious about having never known a black person. After I mumbled the introduction, Cecilia backed up a half step and Mary May, my mother, cautiously said: "Hello, are you Silvia's mother? I have been wanting to meet you." They were not sure what they should say. Cecilia started to turn her head sideways and smiled nervously. Mary May, usually a good conversationalist, smiled and looked to me. The conversation had ended.

"Let's find Silvia's dad so I can introduce you to him," I told my mother. This time there was little nervousness, if for no other reason than there was little communication. Alfonso Silva, who had just given away his daughter in an English language service, spoke no English. When I introduced my mother and him, I mentioned that he had flown from his home in Santurce, Puerto Rico to see Silvia's wedding. My mother picked up the key: "You came all the way from Puerto Rico for the wedding?" she asked. He nodded and smiled. I remarked to the two of them that a father must have a little bit of apprehension when a geographically-distant but emotionally-close daughter asks him to give her hand to someone he has never seen — and never discussed with her in person or by telephone. Mary May agreed, Alfonso smiled again, and the "conversation" ended.

I was almost shocked. Probably awakened is a better word. The difficulty of these introductions illustrated, simply yet dramatically, the differences between my family and culture and that of the bride standing next to me. We had spent two

30

years talking seriously about each other's families, but now this seemed like a mere game of intellectualizing.

I had seen Cecilia a number of times, and Silvia had lived for ten days with my parents in Iowa. I looked at my parents on one side of the church and then looked at Silvia's on the other side. When I had seen Cecilia previously, I recognized differences between her and my parents, but explained these in terms of their very different environments. When Silvia visited my parents, she saw differences between them and her parents, but she too expected this. A non-working housewife living in a middle class home naturally has more time and resources to prepare supper than does her mother. But on this wedding day, everybody was under the same roof, there were no differences of physical environment to detract from the more important human differences of race, religion, language, and economics. The differences between our families were not merely a product of their different environments. The lesson seemed obvious now, but we had overlooked it for two years.

Silvia's and my visit to Iowa had been in June, 1964. In May, soon after we said we were planning to be married, my mother suggested — as she probably would have done in the case of any proposed marriage — that the prospective groom bring his prospective bride home to see his parents. As we boarded our 727 at John F. Kennedy Airport, Silvia was beginning the first vacation she had ever had; and I considered myself a little bit benevolent for making it possible, irrespective of my self-interest in the whole thing. Her only other flight had been an ordeal — the overloaded night flight bringing her mother and her from Puerto Rico. So she was a little bit apprehensive about the flight, although not about the visit. At least if she was, she didn't talk about it.

I know I had no apprehension. I was looking forward to it! Not only was I the would-be husband showing off his fiance to mom and dad, but I was proud of the exhibit. I found her particularly interesting because she was different. My dad spotted this, knowing that his nonconformist son sometimes did things because they were unpopular, not necessarily because he wanted to do them. After eight or nine "get-acquainted days,"

31

he questioned me briefly about a biracial marriage. He, like me, was liberal and idealistic. Unlike me, he was cautious, realistic, fearful.

"I know you want to marry her," he said. "What I want to know is would you marry her if she weren't black?"

I resented this question, mostly because it was a good one. I was mad and unsure as I began my answer. I could enjoy the challenge of a bigot attacking interracial marriage, I could enjoy the praise of an integrationist praising the virtues of interracial marriage, I could enjoy sympathizing with someone puzzled as to why black would want to marry white. But I did not enjoy responding to my father's question. Rather than answering yes or no, I tried to tell him he shouldn't ask the question. I said I wanted to marry Silvia regardless of her color. Finally I admitted I might want to marry her a little bit more because she was black. Maybe my desire to marry Silvia was stimulated by hopes of wrath from the bigot, praise from the integrationist, and questions from the puzzled.

At the wedding, dad was his usual quiet self, talking to few people and keeping his thoughts within. I turned from the two sets of parents, all of whom seemed different from me, to the bride who seemed very similar to me. For good or for bad, we were standing in the doorway. Next to the doorway was a stand, the sort usually used to hold the guestbook at weddings. We had forgotten to get one, but if we had had one, it would have recorded names of very diverse people. Jon Amsel, the upper-middle-class Jewish friend from Connecticut, was not the only one who had reason to feel a little out of place.

"Pat! Here's a lady I'd like you to meet," Silvia said to me soon after the service. As she directed me toward the woman and attracted her attention, she said: "This is Mrs. Richardson. She was very friendly to me when I first came to this country."

"Oh, yes. Silvia told me how you had helped her," I said as I greeted Mrs. Richardson.

Soon after Silvia had come to New York, she had noticed on her way to school in Harlem Mrs. Hortess Oakley Richardson. Silvia liked her broad smile. She began to look for her on her way home from school, she had told me. Several meetings later,

Mrs. Richardson said "Hi," but Silvia said she didn't speak English. A few days later, Mrs. Richardson pointed to her apartment, inviting Silvia to visit, but Silvia declined as her mother had told her to do in the case of such invitations. Not giving up, Mrs. Richardson found a translator and went with her to the apartment where Silvia and her mother stayed. This led Cecilia to permit visits to Mrs. Richardson's comfortable Harlem apartment, a pleasant contrast to those where she had been living.

Another guest was Adelaine Abrams. Silvia was surprised to see her at the wedding. They had worked together in the book-keeping department of a dress manufacturer in the garment district, where Silvia had supported herself and worked her way through college. "Seeing her," Silvia said later, "reminded me of how big a struggle it had been. She had been very friendly and motherly to me."

Then Silvia visited with India Frey. "Seeing her reminded me of the hard time of going through Brooklyn College and the achievement of having finally made it," she said later. The classes they took together included an introductory mathematics course, where she met Bob Frey. Bob, a writer, and India, an English major, rivaled Silvia's inability at mathematics. The most important equation from the class was $1+1=2$, a bi-racial marriage between black India and Jewish Bob.

I started looking for Father Sullivan, failed to find him, and then asked Silvia if she had seen him. She said no, and I asked her where priests usually went after the service, because I wanted to thank him for the way in which he had counseled us and had conducted the service. "And what about paying him?" I asked Silvia with concern.

"I asked him about that the last time you asked me about it, but he said to wait until after the service. Don't worry about it."

I was concerned, because I recognized I had a debt and had been taught to feel uncomfortable until a debt is paid. But I wasn't in a mood to worry.

Fortuantely Father Sullivan had not left until he and my father had met each other. They exchanged brief pleasantries, which since I knew each, I knew each meant. Living in a com-

33

munity that was ninety-five percent Protestant, dad worked hard at being free of religious bigotry. That did not oblige him to lessen his convictions that Protestantism was better — at least for him and probably for his son — than was Catholicism. I suspected he came to a Catholic Church expecting the ceremony of the Catholic masses he had seen on television. I could sense his relief as he told me after the wedding how practical and inspiring he found Father Sullivan's service.

Now that the service was over, it was time for the lighter side of the marriage day. Silvia and I were ready to walk through the doorway. Our first trip as newlyweds was to be measured in miles, and we knew it was to end up at a reception in the Forest Hills section of Queens. The more symbolic trip was to be measured in union and disunion between us, and we were confident it was to end up in a happier life for each of us.

We walked together toward my 1964 Plymouth which I had gotten two months earlier, soon after moving to Huntington Station, New York to start reporting for *Newsday*, Long Island's largest daily. I had learned from my mother to be suspicious of those who made a big thing about such matters as new cars for weddings, rather than concerning themselves with the more important aspects of the relationship. I had not gotten this car for my marriage, but for my work. I was glad, however, that by coincidence our wedding car was a new one: it symbolized the brightness of our wedding day and the emotional energy we had accumulated for the long trip we were about to take together.

As I held the door for Silvia, joking that this would not be the most appropriate time to forget to do so, the door and the rest of the car was free of the whipped cream and other markings that frequently decorate the car of the newlyweds. As we pulled away, there were no tin cans banging behind. I commented that the lack of trivia was typical of our relationship. We had met, not at a social event, but at a narcotics center.

It was 1963. The scene was the Lower East Side Narcotics Center in Manhattan. I was researching a magazine article on narcotics. The Columbia Journalism School requires a magazine-type article as a master's thesis; and I had decided to write

34

about drugs, since the only time I'd heard about them was in a Sunday School Youth Fellowship lesson while in high school. After visiting several centers, I had decided to concentrate on this particular one. Working at the center was very enjoyable to me, even though the subject was even more foreign to me than the low income, interracial housing that surrounded it. This was not the relaxed life of Clarksville, Iowa, the intellectual isolation of Grinnell College, or the campus of Columbia University. It was different, and for that reason it was exciting and challenging to try to understand it. I admired any "normal" person who would venture to work in such a hostile environment with such a vicious problem.

I admired such people so much that I decided that this might be a place to look for a date who, like me, was more interested in human problems than in human pleasures. I wanted someone who was not an addict and who was attending college, which narrowed the field to three or four at this particular place. After thinking briefly about one other girl, I decided to ask out the only black girl who fell within my guidelines. I had always wanted to have a date with a black, and had never had it, so I decided that March 4, 1963 was the time to ask. Her name was Silvia Silva. She worked on a volunteer basis there while attending Brooklyn College part-time and supporting herself with a bookkeeping job.

I usually was a little nervous when making a date, but this time the date was a sociological experiment and so was nothing about which to be nervous. Silvia was nervous since she did not have any idea I would ask her out, as she told me later. She did not indicate this, however, and offered a composed yes — along with her usual smile.

I expected that she might live in an unfavorable neighborhood, so I had no reservation when she started explaining where I would have to go to pick her up.

"It's kind of hard to get to where I live," she told me as she gave directions.

Thanks to the directions and to starting out two hours ahead of time, I got to her Bushwick Avenue apartment on time. She said months later that she had rehearsed the introductions she

35

made once I got into the two-room apartment: "I'd like you to meet my mother, Cecilia Green," Silvia said. Never good at meeting people, I had a particularly hard time here because I could tell that Cecilia was as nervous as I, and that she felt very uncomfortable speaking English.

"This is her husband, Tom," Silvia continued. Tom smiled and we greeted each other without hesitation. He was more like me, being white and the product of a small Missouri town. He may have had more in common with me than with Cecilia, since their basic similarity was pretty much limited to the fact they both happened to be poor and lived in the same apartment building, where he was janitor. Silvia then introduced me to their daughter, Hilda; and the dates left for Broadway, and for *Mutiny On The Bounty*, with Marlon Brando.

Twenty-four months later as we drove toward the wedding reception, we visited about the development of our relationship, about the reasons the first date was not the last. Silvia's mother had suggested to her before the first date that when a white man dates a black woman, he might be more interested in sex than love. Silvia almost cancelled the first date — not for fear of that, however, but because when she got home from work that Friday a notice of dispossession had been served on them, giving them four days to vacate the apartment. "I was upset because I had given my mother the money to pay the rent and she had not paid all of it," she explained later. "I didn't feel like socializing."

That first date, like this first ride after our marriage, was relaxed, serious, and happy. Our racial and cultural differences made the first date easier for me, and probably for her, than a date between people of similar background, because each of us wanted to find out more about other peoples' cultures. Throughout our courtship, our differences in background were not barriers to conversation but rather stimulants to it.

We had not gone very many minutes into that first date without realizing that we had much in common. I was the angry young man denouncing the social ills of society; and she enjoyed this, if for no other reason than she had sometimes been the victim of society. She told me she wanted to be a social

36

worker "because my family has had some problems and I want to do something to help people." This sounded like my junior high Sunday School teacher, and so I was impressed with Silvia, particularly with her doing volunteer work while at the same time working for a living and going to college.

As we drove toward the reception, I was thankful that during the first date I decided that rather than a one-time experiment with a black date, the event was interesting enough to be repeated, particularly since I was not interested in anyone else at the time. I decided that although marriage was always possible, our dating would not be "wasted" even if we only dated a few times, since it would be educational for both of us and we would have a good time while learning. Besides that, I knew I was giving her an opportunity to eat a better meal than she got the rest of the week and a little entertainment she might not be able to afford.

It did not take more than three or four dates for us both to realize that although we weren't going to jump into marriage, we were serious. In March, when I started looking for jobs available upon my graduation in June, I largely limited my search to the New York area so I could live near Silvia.

Most of our dates were centered around a moderate-priced Saturday night meal in midtown Manhattan, a meal lasting sixty or seventy mintues because of our long and serious conversations about social and political matters. The same subjects dominated our conversations during our extensive walking around Manhattan, while entertainment included movies, off-Broadway plays, visits to public museums and parks, and Brooklyn Sociology Club lectures and parties.

Dates included visits to a variety of churches. When Silvia told me on our first date that she was Puerto Rican, my enthusiasm for her lessened as I said: "Are you a Roman Catholic, like most Puerto Ricans?"

She said yes, but lessened my concern about this matter as she indicated she was not as rigid in her theology as I thought most Catholics to be. Since my previous opportunity for religious diversity had been limited by a predominantly middle-road Protestant home town and a Protestant and Jewish undergraduate college environment, I wanted to be exposed to other religions while in New York City. Having been limited primarily to a Catholic environment, she liked my suggestion of attending various churches together. Our favorite ended up being Riverside Church, a large, liberal nondenominational church built with Rockefeller money near Columbia University.

We had talked about religion a great deal and agreed it would be presumptuous of either of us to say his religion was right and the other's was wrong. We agreed to consider becoming a member of each other's church but not feel obligated to do so. The church we had just been married in was Catholic because I told Silvia that regardless of what religion either of us ultimately adopted, her mother would probably feel better if she were married as a Catholic.

Soon after we drove into Queens that wedding afternoon, we visited briefly about the unexpectedly delightful time we had had at the 1964 World's Fair there. The spectacle was a first for each of us, and that made it all the more enjoyable. We enjoyed it slightly more because we were biracial, since this gave us the incentive to do such things as listen to the Mormon Church's view of interracial marriage as expressed at its exhibit at the fair.

As with the World's Fair, our dates were often made just a little more interesting because of our being biracial. Since usually we went to conventional middle class events of the Radio City Music Hall sort, I felt a little tingle of accomplishment in escorting a black woman; but Silvia told me years later that she had no such feeling. The other events we attended, such as off-Broadway plays, usually involved thoughts or people that were left of center, so our being biracial was more of an asset there than a liability.

Our biracialness sometimes added a little humor. On one of our dates soon after I began work in New Jersey, I was to meet Silvia at the home of Judy Rogers, a college friend living with her parents in East Orange. When I went to the door of the home, Mr. Rogers said in a soft-spoken way that I must have the wrong address. I checked the address with him a couple times and asked him if his daughter was having a party. He said yes, he thought so, and went to get her. As she, black like her father,

38

came out to the screened porch where I was standing, she looked a little puzzled. When I asked if she were Silvia's friend, she paused and invited me in. "I never thought to tell her you were white," Silvia joked with me afterward.

As we got to Forest Hills, the landscape was at the opposite end of the economic spectrum from Fort Greene. The reception was at Blanche and Jack Brody's because they were friends of Silvia, and owned the only nice New York City home available to either of us.

"Is this the Forest Hills where the tennis tournaments are held?" I asked Blanche at the reception, since the place was foreign to me except in that regard. Although the area was even more foreign to Silvia, the people were not. In fact, she had gotten to move so easily among socio-economic groups during her college years that she forgot that other members of her culture did not. Several cars of Spanish guests got lost on the way to Brody's, we found out later. "I never stopped to think that they had not been in that area and would not know how to get there," she said later. "I guess I thought that because I'd been there, they'd know how to get there."

Jack was a soft-spoken electrical engineer. Blanche, not soft spoken, had met Silvia in a sociology course they took together.

I had told Silvia we should help do the planning for the reception and pay for it, but Henni Fischer, another Brooklyn College friend, told me: "You just worry about getting married and we'll take care of the reception! O.K."

She and Blanche prepared food and did the planning. A couple who lived in an apartment above Silvia's cooked the turkey, even though they had known her only four months. The reception included a conglomeration of racial, ethnic, and economic backgrounds. Various groups associated with each other, although it was easy to notice that most of the Puerto Ricans were on one side of the living room speaking Spanish to each other and the bride's parents, while the rest of us spoke English.

When someone told me it was time to open the gifts, I discouraged it. I did the same when Silvia made the same suggestion ten minutes later, explaining that I recognized the

39

economic differences represented and did not want to make somebody feel bad because his or her gift was less valuable than someone else's. Silvia saw no need for such an approach, telling me "everybody wants to see what we got."

Soon after the gifts were opened, my dad's brother, Roger, said that he and his daughter had to return home to Montclair, New Jersey, where he was pastor of a large, wealthy Presbyterian Church.

"I certainly wish the best for Silvia and you," he said before saying good-by. I had told him twenty months earlier about my possibly having a biracial marriage, and he said that it was an exciting thought. My dad had talked excitedly about such things, too, when other persons were involved. Maybe that is why I was a little surprised when, in spite of the liberal, almost rebel nature he had inspired in me, he had some reservations once I told him his own son was marrying a black Puerto Rican.

After Roger, the next driver heading toward New Jersey was Tom McDevitt. I had told Silvia there was no point in having any alcoholic beverages at the reception, but she replied: "People expect to have something to drink." Consequently I had turned to Tom and had him do the purchasing. I thanked him for coming and for bringing the liquor, and gave him the bottle that had not been opened.

A few guests were still at the reception, but my mother told me that she and dad were ready to go. This disappointed me because I had not had much time to talk with them since they had arrived a day earlier. Her departing words were specific: "I certainly hope you have had good training in birth control, because with all the other problems of an interracial and interreligious marriage, you don't need any added burdens."

I said thank you and good-by, bothered by the little bit of emotion evident in her usually calm voice. This was the mother I'd always known and usually loved, and the mother who had written to me in May, 1963 about biracial marriage. In the May letter, written after I wrote about my marriage plans, she said:

Naturally you are awaiting a reaction and naturally we have discussed it muchly since your letter arrived. It is fine that you have found someone with whom you can be happy the rest of your life. The prospect of marriage is certainly a thing not to be taken lightly. It is a serious business and not to be easily cast aside. I hope that during the course of this long engagement (and I hope it is a long one) you have much time to discuss the aspects of any marriage and particularly one of mixed faith and mixed race. I know that everything of great value comes from the mind and heart, but we still have to live in this sometimes cruel world and be aware of its challenges. I am sure that you truly feel Silvia to be a fine girl or you wouldn't be interested in her. And your description of the place in which you met rather than a social function is well put. . . The religious angle is of more interest to me than the nationality.

The letter could be abstract and unemotional because it was written twenty-one months in advance of the event. It was now D-Day, and emotion had come from the most unemotional and understanding of parents.

Dad, who also was a little concerned on this wedding day, had limited his comments in that 1963 letter to finances, advising me to make sure I had a salary that could support a marriage.

I definitely had thought about finances. I had lived simply in my bachelor days and expected to continue to do so. I knew my modest living standard was far better than that Silvia had been having, so I assumed her expectations did not surpass mine. Much of that marriage proposal walk from Central Park to Times Square in 1963 had been about money. "I don't want you to think that just because I have a master's degree from a sophisticated college and come from a middle class home that I have a lot of money or expect to make a lot of it. Most newspapermen are paid very little in terms of what comparable education and aggressiveness brings in other professions. I only make about $110 a week now and don't expect that to increase rapidly. Don't take me, if you want money."

Before going to Huntington Station, we took Cecilia to her apartment. Silvia's dad was already at Benedicta's, where he was to stay a week before returning to Puerto Rico. My parents were back at their hotel asleep, preparing for their return flight to Iowa the next morning.

Then Silvia and I began our first trip home to our home. It was not like her mother's low income apartment. It was not like her father's apartment in Puerto Rico. It was not like my

41

parents' comfortable seventeen-year-old frame house surrounded by a half acre of land. We were not like her parents or my parents. What we were like we had to find out.

My salary was now $125 a week, and the Huntington Station apartment toward which we were heading reflected the lack of affluence. In fact, it was the basement of a one-family house — clean, comfortable, but unexciting. But our spirits were rich.

We were riding home, not going on a honeymoon. I had just started work at *Newsday*, so time off for a honeymoon would have been out of the question. That was no problem. I did not want a honeymoon. As I had explained to Silvia a year earlier, I thought a honeymoon vacation might better be taken several months or years after marriage when the magic of marriage has worn off. Right after marriage, a couple could be expected to be happy leading a normal life without such accessories as honeymoon trips. With us, at least, the theory was right. We did not need to travel to recognize the magic of marriage.

"I'll have to admit it was really a great day," I said to Silvia that night.

"It was even better than I thought it would be," she added.

The honeymoon had begun. We had walked through the doorway of the church. We had walked through the doorway of our apartment. We had walked through the doorway.

The honeymoon had begun.

CHAPTER III

The Two-Year Honeymoon

This was Number Four. It was a brisk fall day in 1966, and the clock on the Licking County Courthouse should have just registered 11:00 A.M. as I went to a pay phone to call Silvia at work.

If she was upset by the bad news, she didn't show it. I asked her if she would come and get me, and she said certainly she would. She could leave on her lunch hour in a few minutes.

This was Number Four. The fourth job I'd lost in the twenty months since we'd been married. This time I had asked for it: I had been insubordinate to the city editor of *The Newark Advocate*, a small Ohio daily in this county seat near Columbus where I'd worked a year.

Huntington Station, Long Island; Asbury Park, New Jersey; Gloversville, New York; and now, Newark, Ohio. Four places, three states, two years, one couple. So many jobs and so many different 'hometowns' certainly wasn't the way we had planned things. But despite this abnormal element, our marriage was normal. It certainly seemed to be a happy one — happier than either of us had imagined it could be.

Silvia's unrumpled voice over the telephone was gentle and sympathetic, just as I had expected. She had often proven I could count on her resourcefulness and understanding, regardless of the situation. She knew that regardless of the problem of the moment, I would overcome it. She restated this confidence two weeks later when, while preparing to move to Cincinnati where I had gotten a higher paying job on *The Post*, she said: "I think it is great the way it only took you a week to get another job. That shows you must have something on the ball."

The moving about started a month after we were married. I was unable to obtain a New York driver's license, due to my diabetic and epileptic convulsions, and therefore had to resign from my reporting job at *Newsday*. The next week I got a job on *The Asbury Park Press*, a good daily in New Jersey, where I still had a valid driver's license.

We moved into an unfurnished apartment — without owning any furniture — and both enjoyed sleeping on the floor a few nights, and later telling our friends about it. In a few weeks Silvia had a job in Asbury Park; my one-month trial period with the *Press* ended in my dismissal. I had spent too much time mourning my departure from *Newsday*, rather than doing good work for the *Press*. My father, however, was convinced otherwise, writing a letter to the managing editor asking if my dismissal was related to my diabetes or my wife's color. Silvia and I didn't think her pigmentation or my pancreas were involved, however, and so weren't bothered by my dad's letter.

By then Silvia had learned how to drive. I thought she had done it because she wanted to help us make up for a limitation I couldn't help. I kept this assumption until nine years later when she declared: "I learned to drive because I wanted to be independent."

Regardless of why she learned, it was fortunate that she did. It was she who got our Plymouth to Gloversville, New York, my next place of employment; and she was the only Huber permitted to drive it once we got there.

Gloversville was a quiet small town built on glove making, and suffering from slack in it. The town was relaxed, stable, almost stagnant — a very different environment than that we had had. Long Island had been just the opposite, overcrowded with commuting workers. Asbury Park was crowded, but not with commuters but with tourists, retirees, and local employees determined not to commute to New York City.

Four months later our marriage would be functioning in an even more different environment, rural small-town Ohio. Newark, thirty miles east of Columbus, is a prosperous commercial center for an agricultural area — clean, Protestant, conser-

44

vative, and, of course, predominantly white. There was opposition to the Republican Party there, not because of its conservatism, but rather for its liberalism. In fact, the United States Congressman was John Ashbrooke, who ran for President in 1972 to oppose the leftism of Richard Nixon.

And then there was Cincinnati, which for a biracial couple, for most people, is not small-town Ohio, big-town New York, or anywhere else Pat and Silvia Huber had lived.

Against five different environments the black and white of this marriage was projected, and the screen showed happiness and satisfaction. The biraciality of this marriage strengthened some of its aspects during this two-year honeymoon, weakened almost none, and for the most part seemed a small part of a very happy relationship. How color differences did or didn't affect eleven specific aspects of our life is now discussed on the basis of each aspect:

Finances. The salesman seemed to overlook the unfamiliar sight of a biracial couple walking into a furniture store in Long Branch, New Jersey, and began working immediately to sell us a $400 bedroom set. Our backs had been becoming less fascinated with the novelty of sleeping on the floor of our apartment, so we decided to look. My rule on all expenditures for furniture and appliances was that at our age, each item either be very good, something we would enjoy for decades, or just enough to get by. Silvia didn't question; and I didn't expect her to.

We decided to get good bedroom furniture and had the money in the bank. While preparing to make a deposit to the store, I, in one of my typical attempts at wry humor, turned to Silvia and said: "I guess it doesn't make much difference what amount I put on this check since we only have about $12 in the account anyway."

The salesman didn't laugh. The manager didn't laugh.

"If you would rather wait on the furniture, we can deliver the mattress to you this weekend along with a frame that will hold it until you get a bed," the manager said. Taking the hint, the salesman added: "That will give you a chance to try out the mattress, and then if you want to get the bed and dressers later, you can do that."

45

"A lot of people do it that way," the manager assured us.

We assumed the salesman and manager might not have been so quick to assume our finances were not normal if we had been a more "normal" couple. Anyway, we hadn't been sure we should spend money on a bedroom set, so we weren't bothered. We felt a sense of power being able to laugh inside about the whole thing, taking the attitude: "O.K., so you're suspicious of our being biracial. That's fine, because your ignorance amuses us, and will cost you a sale besides."

April, 1965, Silvia Huber, employed, walked into a leading Asbury Park, New Jersey, bank to start a savings account with a deposit of $18.

I asked her why she started the account.

"I got paid today and didn't need the money, so I thought I should save it." she explained, failing to get my message that regardless of the virtue of saving, it was rather silly to do it $18 at a time.

I didn't attach significance to the savings account being in her name only. Perhaps I should have. Anyway, I figured she had had her mind in the right place when she wanted to save: and all I had to do was educate her as to how to do it in a more expedient manner. She didn't increase the account. If she was bothered by my teasing her about the sixteen-cent interest accrual notice the bank sent her each quarter, she made no such indication.

My personal financial philosophy had long been to spend as little as possible; and I had wanted a spouse that had the same philosophy. I figured this was an advantage of marrying a product of the slums. I found out differently six or seven years later; but in these first two honeymoon years, this seemed to be the case because my conservativeness in spending our middle-class income still offered a much more abundant life than Silvia had experienced prior to our marriage.

Several weeks later we were walking along the Atlantic beach right in front of our apartment, relaxed in spite of my recent dismissal from *The Asbury Park Press*. This was the first illustration of how my (our) savings, plus her employment, kept a disappointment from turning into a financial crisis. She said a couple years later: "You know, I like the way you want to save

46

money even though there doesn't seem to be a need for it at the time."

Silvia seemed to like my philosophy of having money available so that any proposed expenditure was not influenced by whether we had money for it. For example, when Silvia said that year that Benedicta would like to go to school but couldn't because of lack of money, I said: "If we bought her books and paid the tuition, would she want to go?"

A little surprised, Silvia asked: "You mean we could pay it?"

Silvia had been influenced by "poor peoples' budgeting," which determines whether to make an expenditure on the basis of whether the money is available. I said: "If you think it would be a good investment, we have the money to make it."

Two months later Benedicta was enrolled and studying her new books.

Silvia's career. The bride of five months moved to Winooski, Vermont, on July 6, 1965, leaving her husband behind in New Jersey.

"Aren't you afraid what your husband will do when you take off so soon?" asked one of Silvia's fellow students at Saint Michaels's College.

Silvia wasn't worried. She knew we were both happy about what she was doing. She was attending a two-month training session for counselors, which was financed under the Federal Manpower Act of 1962. This training, including later discussion about the teasing of her fellow trainees, united us because it confirmed to us that we were interested in things more important than each other. The unifying effect was particularly strong because Silvia was black, and the training emphasized to us that she was an outstanding contrast to the stereotype of the black woman whose primary concern was lover and children.

Actually, this may have meant a more independent and less traditional wife than even I wanted. If so, I didn't catch the signal. For the time being, at least, the training session symbolized a learning and ambitious Silvia; and that image brought us closer together.

Silvia's job, like that of most wives, was of little concern to her husband. It was of much concern to her.

47

As a follow-up to Winooski, she had on-the-job training in Albany in September, 1965. Then she worked for the New York State Employment Service in Gloversville, continuing there after I'd gone to Ohio.

In Newark in late 1965 she walked into the Ohio Bureau of Employment Services in Newark, through the same doorway, past the same secretary, and into the same waiting room where an interviewer had told her three days earlier there was no job available. This time there was a difference. The publisher's assistant of the local newspaper had eaten supper in our house two nights earlier, had asked Silvia what type of work she did, and said he'd contact his friend who managed the local employment office for the state. On this second visit to the employment service, the manager interviewed Silvia and hired her.

As we discussed delightedly this triumph, we considered it a great example of a biracial couple using the white boss of the white spouse to get for the black spouse a job she should have been considered for in the first place. We felt the system had been beaten, and our biracialness made it possible.

My career. "I know this sounds bad after we haven't seen each other since I left Gloversville a month ago, but I'd rather you didn't come over to my apartment — I mean our apartment — right now. Go find something else to do for an hour or so, like go eat supper if you haven't had it yet, and then it will be O.K. to come. I don't know when I'll be back, probably about 10:30, but when I come, don't run out and greet me."

Silvia was calling from the Newark, Ohio bus station. She had arranged to come to Newark a day ahead of schedule to surprise her new husband, and now he told her not to come home.

"I don't understand. What's the matter, Pat?" she asked with dismay.

Realizing my avoidance of the facts had created the concern in Silvia's mind I had wanted to avoid, I started telling her the facts. "I am going to a John Birch Society meeting tonight. Now don't let that upset you," I added quickly. "Six weeks of rural Ohio hasn't made me an archconservative. It has to do with a story I want to write, but I haven't told anybody. Oh! I think I hear my ride coming in now. Don't worry about any-

48

thing! Just don't greet me when the Society member brings me back home tonight. Better yet, don't leave any lights on in the apartment. They might not trust me as much if they saw your shade. Good-by."

Silvia had had some misgivings about living in the Midwest; and my first communication with her there didn't make her any more relaxed about it. She didn't tell me until the 1970's how frightened she was as she looked for our apartment that night. She did find it, and I got home safely and began explaining. I had the best story of my career brewing, and I didn't want my wife's color to complicate matters. I had attended several monthly meetings of a local chapter of the John Birch Society, pretending to have a genuine interest in that rightwing group that conducted all its meetings in secret, while in fact I wanted to find out the extent and nature of its local membership and their plans for the future.

A month later, when a Society member came to pick me up for the next meeting, I told Silvia to get in the bathroom and turn on the shower so my chauffeur wouldn't ask to meet her. I didn't realize at the time that this worried Silvia, nor did I realize how much she and my parents were worried about an incident a month after that. In order to save my usual chauffeur the trouble of picking me up, I decided to have my parents take me to the home where the next meeting was scheduled. After I had gotten out of the car and walked toward the house, one of the members said he'd like to meet my parents.

I made up an excuse to go back to the car alone and quickly told Silvia to lie down in the back seat so she wouldn't be seen. The Society member came to the car, met my parents, and did not see Silvia, so I thought everything was all right. Silvia said later, however: "My heart was pumping so hard I thought they could hear it. Your dad asked me as we drove away if I thought it was safe for you to be with these people. He didn't need my fears to add to his own, so the only thing I could say was nothing. Finally your mother said: 'It must be safe for him to go there or he wouldn't do it.'"

Once the paper printed my four-part series on the Birch Society, I was proud, and she was proud and relieved. We enjoyed it even more than we otherwise would because anti-black sentiment was exposed in the series — sentiment we both disliked but which could have been reported only if at least one of us was white.

My reporting in Newark drew us closer together because I was our mouthpiece for those convictions we shared. We both liked the fact that because of me, the NAACP in Newark was recognized by the press. We, along with our friends, enjoyed my reporting that the local office of President Johnson's War On Poverty program had spent money but done nothing, and that the local establishment seemed happy that nothing had been done except pay bureaucrats' salaries.

My bad reporting as well as my good reporting united us, the best example being a story about a right-wing black woman, formerly an FBI agent, who had been invited to speak locally, largely through the support of Birch Society members. Leaving aside my typical crime of getting to the speech after it started, I committed numerous journalistic sins and wrote an unobjective story. I went too far to try to show the woman was a screwball. Our marriage, however, was affected not by the poor journalism, but by our recognition that I had tried to put the woman's speech into perspective, challenging her contention that she spoke for the majority of blacks in the nation.

Despite the limited satisfaction of Newark reporting, my career was on the downgrade. It had been since our marriage, because when our marriage began I was at *Newsday*, the height of my career. There, in addition to working for the best suburban daily in the country, I had a managing editor, Bill McIlwain, whom I respected for his personal as well as his professional qualities. This added to the hurt of leaving *Newsday*. The downtrend seemed to continue at Newark.

Although my primary concern was my career, I did not think of relating my professional disappointment to my wife. In fact, my career problems seemed to unite us because we joined to meet the challenge of the next move and the next job. Our biraciality was a small factor, but helped, because we were the couple that expected challenges.

Now I see that our biracialness contributed to my failure. It helped make me too much a reformer in reporting social, political, and racial issues to write what the establishment wanted to read. But at the time I saw no way in which our biracialness was affecting my career, and no way in which our marriage was affecting it, so I did not penalize the marriage. My drop from *Newsday* hurt, but I was the man falling from the skyscraper who had received no injuries as he fell past the first few stories. I had not yet hit the sidewalk, and until then, neither I nor the marriage would feel the pain.

Friends. The Hubers didn't have many friends in Huntington Station and Asbury Park; and that proves nothing, given the brevity of their residency. In Gloversville, I felt at home because it was like my hometown; and Silvia did not feel at home because it was not like her hometown. I didn't bother to make friends, and she found hers where she worked. We were still too much interested in each other to be concerned about friends or the lack thereof.

Newark, Ohio is not exactly bulging with interracial couples or those experienced in associating with them. This didn't bother us; it made us feel interesting. We enjoyed associating with many who enjoyed our friendship and others more interested in our uniqueness, and were too secure to be bothered by anyone who did not want to associate with an interracial couple. In fact, we enjoyed laughing at those whom we considered too bigoted to fraternize with us. We also enjoyed analyzing a few social conversations. For example, we wondered if the former southerner eating in our home who told all the clever jokes about "dumb Polacks" might at times have told the same jokes with the role of the fool played by another ethnic group frequently residing in his homeland.

Our Newark friends included the director of the local NAACP, whom I liked and about whom I had written two newspaper stories — probably the first stories *The Newark Advocate* carried about that little band. Other than he and his wife, almost all our friends were white. Silvia didn't complain — there was little alternative; and I did not recognize the significance of the situation at that time, although eight years later I would. I didn't stop to realize in Newark that when black and Spanish

51

become more accessible as friends, my black and Spanish wife would want to associate with them — probably more than with whites, while I would want to continue to associate primarily with whites.

Our focus at the time, however, was on the many good friends we made there, some of them from our respective jobs, and the majority from the academic community of nearby Dennison University.

Barbara Lotz and her husband, Bill, an engineer at the Owens Corning Factory in Newark, met Silvia at an NAACP meeting and invited us to visit them that weekend at their nearby farm. We kept going back, weekend after weekend. We enjoyed their four preteen children, their intelligence, their friendliness, their liberalism. I helped Bill paint his house, and Barbara gave Silvia a lesson in how to raise potted plants. Both the gal from New York City and the boy from Iowa needed a lesson on how to milk the family cow. Barbara and Bill, both white, told us about their thoughts of adopting a biracial youngster.

In Cincinnati, somebody told Silvia at work about a biracial couple and suggested we might get together. We did, laughing somewhat about how biracial couples apparently were recognizable enough in Cincinnati that one was referred to another. We visited that couple only once, having little in common with them other than our biracialness. Silvia recruited us several good friends in Cincinnati, but we both were a little unsure as to how welcome we might be in some white homes, and a little arrogant as to whether the socio-intellectual capacities of some blacks justified our attention.

Religion. The Presbyterian Church in the Newark, Ohio area was not used to seeing stories on the front page of the local newspaper about the meetings of its Presbytery — the church's next highest ruling body above the local church. Particularly alarming was this story in early 1966 because it was not conventional. That might be because Pat Huber wrote it.

The story was about a restrained exchange of opinion between the guest speaker, a New York City minister, and an Ohio minister questioning his having permitted in his church the

52

presentation of a play which included nude actors.

After I retold the exchange to Silvia that night, we were highly critical of the Ohio minister for being so concerned about the nudity issue he ignored what the minister said in his inspiring keynote to the meeting. We also condemned the Ohio minister as being unable to imagine the positive effects the particular play might have had.

That converstation between us reflected our attitude toward religion during our first two years beyond the altar. We regretted the tendency of organized religions to be more concerned about their traditional dogmas and beliefs than about meeting the needs of mankind. In fact, we looked for opportunities to accuse traditional religions of failing to follow the spirit of their religion. This "game" of what's wrong with religion had a certain unifying effect on our marriage, particularly its biracial aspect, since much of the criticism of established religion involved, too, a criticism of racism.

At the same time, I held fast to my religious convictions and urged our attending church. In Newark I read the church page of the *Advocate* to see what sermon topic might be most beneficial that Sunday. We continued our pre-marital policy of attending a variety of churches, partly out of a conviction that we should find out what each has to offer, and partly because this made it unnecessary for us to choose between her Catholic and my Presbyterian heritage.

Ideals. "Well! What would you expect?" Silvia said to me in Cincinnati in early 1967, after my telling her how tough I'd found the United States Undersecretary of State for Far Eastern Affairs. In an interview just finished that evening for the *Post*, I had tried to get him to state what the United States could do to increase the possibility of detente between the East and West. He would not budge, of course, from his contention that the United States had already done more than its share toward this end.

Silvia's and my political and social philosophies seemed to agree almost all the time, while our approaches differed. She would never have challenged a high-ranking state department official. She was cautious and realistic, while I expected great

53

revelations and the overnight transformation of the world. But we were not bothered by our different strategies — merely happy that we wanted the same ends. We agreed that Johnson should change his policy in Vietnam; but we liked his War on Poverty. It was 1967, and that was part of the 1960's, and at age twenty-six we still had the idealism and activism that characterized the spirit of college students in that decade.

Some of our idealism was independent of our biracialness. When it came to racial issues, our idealism was increased by our biracialness, and our marriage was strengthened by its being biracial. We had not noticed much discrimination against us, but what existed united us. Of greater importance was racial discrimination against others. We had fun discussing examples each of us found of it each place we lived, and what we read of it in the newspapers. The most dramatic was in Cincinnati, the first time we had lived in a city while it was experiencing a race riot.

Rather than spend all our time talking about a racial controversy we could do nothing about, Silvia's practical and cautious inclination led her to suggest we play Big Brother to two boys. It sounded humanitarian to me, so I encouraged it. Our two or three visits with them may not have helped them, but it united us. We would have gained satisfaction from helping any disadvantaged youth, but our biracialness gave us additional satisfaction because both of the boys were black.

And there was the case of the concrete replicas of black doormen being sold as they had long been in Newark, Ohio. Suddenly one morning their faces were white. Maybe not a big triumph for racial equality, but enough to make this interracial couple feel even closer together, particularly since we happened to know who did the paint work.

Sex. First of all, let's get the facts correct. Silvia was only a couple of rooms away from the bed where the woman and I were; and the woman was really not in bed with me, and I was just leaning on it. The apartment — dim oriental lights, soft music, and gentle colors — was enticing. More enticing was my hostess — or I guess I should say our hostess — black eyes, brown skin, trim figure, and soft voice. She had just shown me pictures taken of her in her work as a professional model. I particularly liked the one for the soap commercial showing her taking a bath.

Anyway, I had little opportunity to prove the strength of my Puritan values, for we were influenced by the fact that our spouses were in the same apartment that 1966 evening in Cincinnati, Ohio. I didn't get to see any more of her than shown in the soap commercial and in the messed-up chalk portrait she gave me.

She, her husband, Silvia, and I then spent twenty minutes discussing a variety of topics, including Cincinnati's race riots; and then the Hubers went home to their nearby apartment.

"I couldn't believe what I saw," Silvia said in an amazed yet amused voice as we rode home. "I said to myself: 'That couldn't be Pat.'"

We were both amazed and amused. We could enjoy discussing the incident because it was so unlike what either of us had experienced or would experience in the future. We had a very enjoyable sexual relationship with each other and never thought of looking elsewhere. We had never had a problem in our sexual relationship greater than that of our squeaky bed in the Long Island apartment where we began our married life. We started there as two virgins learning together about the matter of sex. Our fascination about the differences between our bodies had been increased by the color difference, but skin pigmentation was usually the least of our interests.

I kidded Silvia a few times that her being more sexually aggressive than I confirmed the stereotype that blacks were wild about sex. But in fact, our racial difference had little affect on our sex life, a sex life that was always satisfying.

Language. I told Silvia during our engagement that if we were to get married, I would want to learn Spanish, both because of the great extent to which this would facilitate communication with her relatives and friends, and because any bright young man should want to learn at least one language besides his own. Since I had stumbled through two years of college French, I would make up for my inability there by taking advantage of living with someone who spoke fluently another language.

55

Not many months beyond the wedding date I had come to realize that it is work to learn another language, even when you live with someone who speaks it. I bought a set of Spanish vocabulary cards, and failed to use them. I had already concocted the defense I'd use for ten years: "The one marriage vow I failed to keep was that I'd learn Spanish."

Suburban Long Island, suburban New Jersey, upstate New York, and Ohio all seemed so far removed from the Spanish language — my wife rarely found any use for it — that learning Spanish seemed to be a good thing to postpone if not forget about. The result was that when Silvia was in the presence of her relatives or any other Spanish-speaking people, I would feel isolated. During the early years this did not bother me. I didn't think Silvia would keep anything from me. I assumed the friends or relatives would not be insulted, but rather would recognize I had not had time to learn Spanish.

In-laws. "I think you need her more than she needs you," my father wrote soon after my parents visited us in 1966.

This sentence reflected the fact that he, like I, had assumed from the beginning that Silvia was the one who would benefit from our marriage and I was the one who was making a sacrifice — a willing sacrifice but a sacrifice nonetheless. My paternalistic or self sacrificial attitude caused no problem between us during those early years, because I kept it to myself. Silvia was just a little insulted by dad's letter, however, because she could not understand or justify his having previously considered her the beneficiary of our marriage. I had understood and justified his position. Consequently, the change in it reflected by this letter was encouraging to me. Now, without prompting, dad had said my wife was a strong asset to his son's marriage. And since he led our family, I knew that meant mother was convinced, particularly since her major worry about me — my health — was lessened now that Silvia had proven that she could effectively jam a clothespin in my mouth during a diabetic or epileptic convulsion.

It wasn't long after we were married before Silvia expressed concern about the relationship between her own mother and Hilda, Cecilia's and Tom's daughter. In early 1966, seeing an

56

opportunity to do something helpful and feeling a moral obligation to take advantage of such opportunity, I suggested that Hilda visit us in Ohio. I said that it wouldn't hurt us to buy the round-trip bus ticket from New York, and that both she and Silvia might like seeing each other for a while in an environment different from that in which they had ever been together. Silvia didn't think the small town middle class environment had as much magic as I thought it did, but said that she would ask her mother if Hilda could come.

I felt benevolent at having initiated the visit. The problem, however, was that once Hilda got there I didn't do anything more. Hilda was bored and out of place, and she returned before the visit had time to affect her — or our marriage.

Hilda's color was closer to mine than to Silvia's, but she was much closer to Silvia culturally. Even when black Spanish wife and white German husband understand each other, they are at a disadvantage when they try to understand each other's families. When the challenge of the differences in families was met, the accomplishment was heightened because of our biracialism. But usually the accomplishment did not occur, although the extent of the failure would not become evident until later years.

My parents made sure they did not see us frequently and seem to be watching over our shoulder. Silvia's mother and sisters didn't see much of us, if for no other reason than that we were far away from them most of the time, and they did not have the money to travel to us. Consequently, neither of our relatives were a particular factor in the early years of our marriage, because we rarely saw them.

Geographically isolated from both sets of relatives, we had little to do with them, and to me that was desirable. I made the mistake of assuming that Silvia agreed; and she made the mistake of not realizing how much she disagreed. She was too practical to demand cross-country trips to see her relatives; and I thought this meant that she had no time for the extended family concept maintained by Spanish and some black people. Three years later, however, when our child came to us and we returned to New York, both of us would see how much Silvia really believed in the extended family.

Homeland. The young man from the midwest plains went a

courting a New York lass. And why a young lady from there? For the same reason that he decided to do his graduate work at an establishment four blocks west of the Hudson River, two blocks east of Harlem, and sixty blocks north of Times Square. Columbia University, Northwestern University, and the University of Missouri were the three best journalism schools in the nation — or at least so said some folks; but this journalism student, admitted to each of them, picked Columbia for the same reason he picked the Brooklyn lass: — he wanted to learn about the world beyond the homeland.

And this gal who lived along Buschwick Avenue had a good time not only walking along Broadway with this lad from those plains where she'd never been, but going to such foreign places with him as Protestant churches, small-town school board meetings, and WASP neighborhoods.

This lad and lass were looking for something different in 1965 and 1966, as they had been in 1963 and 1964, so they weren't bothered about being from their home territory. They were seeing. They were learning. They liked it. They enjoyed going to a different place, being the "different" couple, meeting the "different" friends, and expressing the different ideas. The homeland was far away during these honeymoon years, worth remembering but no place to which they would want to return — they thought.

Us. It had been so taken for granted during the first seven or eight months it had not seemed worth mentioning, but after ten months, we couldn't help but comment to each other that the honeymoon atmosphere typical of the first few months of most marriages was becoming a way of life for us. We noted the absence of any arguments, our automatic tendency to do all things, serious or for fun, together, our regular agreement as to what we should do, and our complete openness with each other.

We agreed there was no reason our entire marriage likely would be anything but a honeymoon. "But," I cautioned, "there will be times when I hate you and times when you hate me."

Silvia's black eyes opened wider than usual. She jerked her head nervously, then mumbled: "No. That won't happen. I
58

couldn't ever hate you. Do you really mean you think you'll hate me sometimes?"

Realizing her concern, I spoke softly, saying: "I hope you didn't think I thought there was something wrong in our marriage when you heard me say that. That is not at all the case. It's just that I suspect there is no human relationship in which the parties always love each other, and I think we should avoid future disappointments by not expecting perpetual bliss in our relationship."

She was not convinced, but she thought about it. Whether I was being realistic or cynical, unfortunately I was right; but we wouldn't find that out for years. In those first two years, the only tension between us occured several months later when, after she tried to tickle me, I slapped her. Her cheek was not injured, but her pride was greatly maligned. She told me that when a man hit his wife, it showed he had no respect for her. I told her to keep the incident in perspective, but she ended up going to work early and deliberately failing to tell me she was going elsewhere in Ohio on a business trip, which left me home that evening wondering what had happened to her. We then agreed that we didn't want such friction.

Typical of our first two years of marriage was her first Christmas note to me in 1965:

. . . As I've told you before, Christmas is a time of year when I think back and evaluate the year. That is, an evaluation of myself relative to those I love, my work and goals in life. Well, what I'm trying to say is that I'm happy. I find that this is one year's end in which I can count numerous blessings. I want to wish you as good a year as I've had. I only hope that I have given you as much as you have given me. My best wishes for next year and all others to come, and may every year which marks Christ's birth add to and perpetuate what we feel for each other. I could probably go on for several pages, but I'll stop here. . . You know how sentimental I can get and I know you don't like that. I can cry just as much when I'm happy as when I'm sad. Today I'm particularly glad although there is nothing here except you to make it seem like Christmas.

CHAPTER IV

The Louisville Affair

It all started out very undramatically. It was April 18, 1967. Since it was Tuesday, it was my day off work at *The Cincinnati Post*, so I spent most of the day reading, loafing, and studying for a graduate course in Russian History I was taking at the University of Cincinnati, just a block from our apartment. The apartment was very nice for $130 a month, perhaps part of the reason we spent almost all our time there.

After Silvia got home from her job at Cincinnati's Youth Opportunity Center, we ate together at home, as usual, and watched the TV news, as usual. There wasn't anything exciting on the news, although we noticed some pictures of a civil rights demonstration in Louisville, Kentucky, led by the Reverend A.D. King, brother of the Reverend Martin Luther King. I pointed out to Silvia that Louisville wasn't so far away, and maybe we should consider participating since we had never done anything in support of racial equality. Silvia, surprised at the suggestion, said she didn't think we should participate.

Friday, April 21 was no more exciting. Silvia had been in Cleveland Wednesday and Thursday for a training session, but we were both home Friday and ate dinner in our apartment after work. The news that night included more pictures of open housing demonstrations in Louisville and reports that 500 to 600 demonstrators had been arrested. Demonstration leaders threatened to tie up Louisville during the Kentucky Derby weekend, the city's most lucrative of the year, unless open housing legislation was passed. I said that since we had not been involved in any social matters, and since we had an obligation to support our beliefs, maybe this was a good opportunity to stand up for what we said.

"I hope the demonstration is a success," Silvia said, "but I don't think we should participate."

I said I had been extremely careful to protect my objectivity as a newspaperman by avoiding participation in any activity with the slightest social or political overtone; but the Louisville situation provided a rare opportunity to exercise social consciousness and maintain journalistic objectivity, because Louisville was far removed and its happenings were not those of Cincinnati.

Silvia said she was bothered by the way the demonstrators were treated and thought it would be safer to stay at home. I said if she changed her mind, she should call me at work the next morning.

April 22. It started like a normal Saturday. I caught the bus on Ravine Street about 5:00 A.M. to go to work, since Saturday's deadlines were earlier.

About 11:00 A.M. I left the copy editors' "rim" to take a phone call.

"Are you still interested in going to Louisville," Silvia said with un-Silvia-like excitement. "I decided I'd like to go."

Surprised, I said yes I was interested, but asked why she suddenly became so interested.

"These people here make me mad. I've been talking to some blacks and they couldn't care less about the demonstration. [She was calling from Xavier University where she was taking a course in the psychology of delinquency.] A girl friend of mine introduced me after class to a friend of hers. He started talking about his plans to go with some friends to the Kentucky Derby. I asked him if he hadn't heard they were boycotting the derby and he said he did, but wouldn't let that upset his plans. And, my girl friend, she didn't even know about the boycott."

"So what do you want to do?" I asked.

"I can make a lunch for us and pick you up after work. Is that O.K.?"

I said it was, and suggested that if we were going to drive that far, we should recruit some people to go with us.

61

"I'll try," she said, "but I know none of my friends here at school will want to go."

Soon after walking back to the rim, I approached James Brooks (that's not his real name), who was 21, single, and the only black I knew at the *Post*, and told him he was welcome to go with us. He didn't seem much more interested than he had when I'd suggested the idea earlier in the week, but finally he said he would go.

The drive to Louisville was enjoyable. To me it had the feeling of a small crusade and a weekend vacation combined. Silvia enjoyed the ride but was still too apprehensive to consider it a vacation. And her apprehension was not just that we were going to a demonstration. Part of it was the mere fact that this was her first trip into a southern border state. Going into Kentucky has emotional impact for a black person that a white spouse might not stop to think about. I hadn't been in Kentucky since I was a kid, but I knew that the people on one side of the Ohio River were just as good as those on the other side. Silvia's image of the south was that created by the racial strife there during the 1960's. To her, going to do something in Kentucky, particularly going to a civil rights march, was not like doing the same thing in Manhattan.

Silvia thanked me for calling the demonstration to her attention. She explained that after hearing the male student say he supported the goals of the demonstration but didn't want to sacrifice going to the Derby, she decided she had really taken about the same position Friday night. "I felt bad," she said, "that it was you who were encouraging our going and I was the one discouraging it. I feel good now, because we *are* doing something for The Cause."

Jim ate the lunch Silvia had made for him, and although he didn't say much along the way, we assumed he was looking forward to Louisville as we were.

Except for our moving and one visit to my parents, we had not taken a trip together since our marriage, even for a weekend. That made it a little more enjoyable.

"Look at that landscape! " I said a few miles outside Louisville. "That must be the Kentucky bluegrass that's so famous.

They have good reason to tell everybody it looks beautiful."

Silvia agreed. But more important than the grass of the countryside was the issue in the city. On the outskirts I told Silvia to stop so that I could call the wire services to find out where the demonstration was to start. Both the Associated Press and United Press International told me that that night's starting point had not been announced, and that it was being changed from night to night. We continued to go on into Louisville. Within a few minutes the black radio station to which we were listening announced the name and address of a church where the demonstration was to start in a few minutes. We got there as quickly as possible, although a little late. We were curious as we walked toward the church, and excited once we got in. We hardly could squeeze in the small church because little standing room was left.

Most of the ideas expressed we had heard before, but never had we heard them expressed so effectively. And rather than making long speeches, each leader would quickly state his message and then turn the podium to someone else: a soft speaker, a loud speaker, a young one, an old one. I particularly remember Hosea Williams referring to the whites' fear of integration producing biracial children, then saying indignantly: "Oh yes. That's a favorite issue of mine. It seems as if the white community is very concerned about that. They seem to forget that it was they who started fathering biracial children, and that for generations black women did not dare to complain about bearing children conceived by their white masters." He then raised his arm, jabbed at his forearm twice and said: "That brown didn't come from Africa."

The march to downtown Louisville was organized as the rally closed, so that those of us to enter the church last were at the front of the march. As the organizers got things ready, we were curious as to how they would go about it. This was a new experience for us, and a very pleasant one as the walk began a few minutes later: it had adventure, the beauty of a spring evening in Louisville, and best of all, a purpose. This purpose made us feel close to those marching with us, even though we knew no one; it made us feel very close to each other, and we told each other so as we walked along. The neighborhood was residential, and no onlookers or police could be seen. We visited continually, noting that a few more people joined in as the march progressed, making about a hundred in all. Some six to ten persons, all black, were in front of us.

Within a few blocks of downtown, the spectators were more numerous than the marchers, but the spectators did not heckle the marchers as onlookers had done earlier in the week in South Louisville. I pointed out men on the streetside wearing yellow hard hats, and Silvia inquired quickly: "Yes. I noticed those. How come they are wearing them?"

"That's so they won't get hurt when the bloodshed starts," I joked, saying that the wearers were probably either cautious newsmen or policemen.

We became curious one or two blocks later when several marchers walked off to the side of the street. A few steps farther a demonstration leader explained that we could pledge to be arrested, or otherwise we should drop out at this point. I said we didn't want to drop out, and Silvia said nothing.

Another half-block and ten or twenty dropouts later, 150 policemen had barricaded the street and lined up like a wall across it.

A policeman said in a matter of fact way: "If you want to drop out, you can go over there to the side."

Silvia, seeing policemen standing like iron statues lined along both sides of the street, yelled to me softly: "Oh Pat, we'd better drop out while he says we can. These people are going to get arrested."

"I don't see any reason why we shouldn't go on," I said. "This is part of it. After all," I smiled, "we did know we'd probably get arrested."

The demonstration leaders knew that about this time Silvia was not the only marcher with second thoughts. They started us singing the classic civil rights song, "We Shall Overcome."

Silvia and I had sung it once or twice before, but this time we had the feeling of what it was all about. Halfway through the first verse, we could see at least one police paddywagon.

"Be limp," yelled a leader as the policemen prepared to make the first arrest of the night. Afterwards we would realize that a limp prisoner was harder to arrest, but at the moment we didn't have time to think. "I can't be limp. I'm scared stiff," Silvia told me. She was the second or third person arrested and booked for parading without a permit and for disorderly conduct, the charges placed on most of the demonstrators. As they put her in the first police wagon, they started to book me.

"What did I do? What are you charging me with? " I asked. "I haven't done anything wrong! "

When asked my name, I again asked with what I was charged. Two cops grabbed me from behind, twisting my arms behind me.

"I'll make him talk," growled a third cop as he grabbed my shirt collar and then began twisting my tie from behind my neck. In three or four minutes the lights of the TV cameras shined on us for about a minute. Some six or seven minutes later, with the cops still choking me, the TV lights shined on us again. "Get in front of that light," one policeman said to a colleague as they twisted the tie tighter, then pushed my arms behind my back up closer to my neck to the point it hurt significantly. I yelled in pain.

"He struck me," shouted the police captain directing the arrests. He jumped back, his cigar dropping to the pavement near his perfectly shined boots.

The subordinate policemen then started roughing me up.

"Hey, that's my husband," yelled Silvia from the nearby wagon as she watched fearfully.

Obviously she was trying to help me; obviously she did not. Being associated with my black wife was not the best formula for leniency. The cops twisted my arms higher toward my neck and I bent down to the pavement. They jabbed me with their nightsticks as I yelled in pain. They quit hitting for a few minutes and then took me to the end of the van, put a billy club against my chest, and threw me in. Silvia was glued to the bench on the van's side as I desperately grabbed for support before banging against the far end. She and the young black sitting beside her were quickly taken to another van.

The police left me alone as they busily booked demonstrators and loaded them into other vans. Later three or four policemen jumped into the van at once as one yelled: "Let's get this one He's been making a lot of noise."

"This is the one that hit the captain," barked another.

They grabbed me by both hands and legs as well as by my waist and pressed me against the floor. They jabbed throughout the body with at least one blow hitting me on top of the head.

"Police brutality! Police brutality!" yelled one of the demonstration leaders. "Let's get a light over here. Get a picture of that."

The ABC cameras proceeded to roll. A picture of them pinning me to the floor of the wagon would appear in Sunday's *Louisville Courier Journal*.

"Shut that guy up," one cop said to several others.

"This guy is making a lot of noise. I'll shut him up," one of them responded as he pushed his hands hard against my throat.

Frightened, perhaps really frightened for the first time in the whole affair, I was having trouble breathing and feared what he was going to do to my mouth. I yelled stop two or three times and then my pleas became unintelligible. After several minutes of this, I decided he was not going to stop. I reviewed my knowledge of law in ten seconds and decided that my mouth was my property, and what happened once he trespassed it was not my responsibility. So. I bit his finger for a moment and then stopped so he could withdraw it. Instead he pushed harder on my mouth and throat. In desparation I bit his finger again, this time hard. He took his fingers out, and two other cops came up and grabbed me and handcuffed me.

As they led me to the front of the van ten or fifteen minutes later for booking, I felt something wet on my head. Sweat, presumed, since I was still hot.

"What can we get on this guy?" the cop doing the booking asked one or two colleagues. They conferred several times and charged me with maiming, a felony, and six misdemeanors. *The New York Times* that Sunday reported it somewhat differently:

"One young white man who had been marching alongside a Negro girl was beaten by three policemen with their nightsticks

66

after a police captain complained that he had been struck. Reporters on the scene said the man had not touched the captain.

"The man was thrown into a police van, where two policemen continued to strike him with their sticks. He was identified as D. Patrick Huber, 26 years old, a copy editor for *The Cincinnati Post*. He was taken to city jail after being treated for head cuts."

Soon I was in an ambulance and at a hospital, where the doctor in the Emergency Room told the police to remove the handcuffs.

Seven stitches were taken in my head, the bleeding was stopped, and I was told I could be bailed out of jail on an emergency basis and left in the hospital. "That won't be necessary," I said, feeling that whatever value an arrest might have would be lessened by staying in the hospital. I said that my only concern was that I have access to insulin and a syringe since I had left mine in our car.

As I rode from the hospital to jail, I felt good because I thought Silvia and I had helped a worthwhile cause. I was confident that she, too, would feel good. In fact, she felt miserable. Taken to jail in the first police van more than an hour earlier, she had been unable to see much of the action, but could hear some of my screams. She anxiously waited to see me as the second van dumped its cargo at the jail. Her worry about me increased when she learned I wasn't in that van either. She frantically asked prisoners brought by the second van if they knew anything about the white man who was beaten.

"I saw him," one of the prisoners said. "They really beat him up badly. They had to take him to the hospital."

Frightened all the more, Silvia wanted to seek information elsewhere. But she was under arrest and in the first group to be put behind bars out of the fifty-three demonstrators arrested that night. She was even frightened by the fingerprinting, the searching, and other jail routines I took for granted.

Each prisoner was allowed to make one telephone call before being locked up. Silvia would liked to have made a dozen calls, but as an alternative she called Benedicta in New York and

67

asked her to contact their mother and call my parents. I would have thought Silvia's call unnecessary — particularly her asking Benedicta to call my parents; but the call later proved to be vital.

When I was brought back from the hospital it was near midnight, but there were 100 or 200 people outside the jail even at that hour as officials went through the process of admitting those arrested. I didn't expect to see Silvia and so was not disappointed when I did not. I assumed she was in her cell, unconcerned about me and glad we had done something for The Cause.

Waiting to be processed, I started eating a battered apple I had carried in my suitcoat pocket, and was interviewed by a reporter — I think he was from the *Courier-Journal*. I told him I was a newspaperman, hoping that would give me some rapport with him. Besides that, I had told Silvia back at our apartment that successful professional people needed to participate in demonstrations to add respectability to them. Another man asked if my head was all right, and I quickly said yes, adding that I had no concern except that I had left my insulin and syringe in our car.

"Don't worry about that. Tell one of the guards you need insulin and he'll see that you get it."

I was naive enough to believe that he was an employee of the jail, seeking to present a good image to the public. Probably he was a member of the open housing group. In any event, his optimism about guards helping me get insulin did not turn out to be justified. I had thought about taking it along in the march, but decided something unordinary might happen and cause it to be broken.

When told of the opportunity to make one telephone call, I was exactly the opposite of Silvia. I did not call anybody because I saw no point in telling my parents or anyone else about a situation they could not change, and which would not be helped by their worry.

After getting locked up around 2:00 A.M., I took a few minutes to greet the five or six prisoners crowded into the same small cell, and was surprised at their lack of response. Particu-

68

larly since most of them were black, I thought they'd appreciate anyone, particularly a white, who had participated in the demonstration. I took my usual dose of anti-convulsant (dillantin and phenobarbitol), and ended my twenty-one hour day by going to sleep quickly, undistracted by the hardness of my narrow bunk bed.

I had a convulsion during the night. It may have been diabetic, caused by the lack of my usual bedtime snack; or maybe it was epileptic, inspired by the unusual events of the evening. As soon as I woke up that morning and asked the guard what I could do to get a dose of insulin, he hardly paid any attention as he busily carried out his many duties, and as he tried to get an over crowded jail ready for breakfast. When he came by later, I asked again.

"Yea, he needs it man. He was sick last night," said a cell mate who had been awakened by the convulsion.

It was ironic. A black prisoner asking the black guard to help out the white prisoner. The guard listened a moment, shrugged his shoulders, and pointed to the many cells he had to attend. He turned away quickly, apparently not wanting to challenge the pleas of me or my fellow prisoner.

As breakfast came into site, it became apparent there was a second problem. My usual breakfast of eggs, cereal, milk, fruit, and toast was not on the menu. The choice was donuts and coffee, or nothing.

Actually the menu was no immediate problem because I knew better than to eat without insulin anyway. Not eating kept me in pretty good shape for an hour or two, but by about 10:00 A.M. or 11:00 A.M., I felt terrible. I made one more half-hearted attempt to convince a guard or supervisor that I needed medicine, but I had no wounds or other obvious indication of medical need, so the man wasn't convinced. I then dropped on my bunk and began waiting — waiting to get sick enough to be noticed.

Eventually, I don't know when, a guard said he was going to take me to the hospital. Once there, a resident asked me what had happened. I told him I needed insulin immediately, but he seemed unconvinced. He spoke differently as soon as the blood tests came back from the lab.

"What's the highest blood sugar you've ever had?" he asked.

One hundred milligrams is normal.

"Mine ranges quite a ways, going from about 70 to 190 in a normal day," I said. "Two or three times when I've been way out of control, though, it's gotten almost to 300. It must be that high now."

He said nothing, left the room quickly, came back in a few minutes, and spoke solemnly: "Your blood sugar was over 700."

A little later another policeman came into the exam room and spoke to the man who had brought me over. "I've got to take this guy back before I can. . .

"I'm not going to let you take him out of here," the doctor interrupted. "He's got to stay here," he said authoritatively, as the policeman started to talk again. The policeman stopped talking.

Silvia rushed up to me at 6:30 P.M. as I was lying on a stretcher waiting to be taken to a hospital room.

"Oh it's so good to see you. I've had a hard time finding you. Are you all right?"

"I'll be O.K. I'm not as bad as I look. All I need is some insulin," I replied.

"I've been so worried about you."

"Really?" I said with disbelief. "There was really nothing to be concerned about. It's just that since I didn't have any insulin, I came the closest to a diabetic coma that I've ever come. But that can be taken care of. My being back here has nothing to do with injuries I got last night."

I talked slowly and with difficulty, Silvia was sensitive to this and so said little even though she had lots she wanted to say. She left within thirty minutes, after I had asked her to call Jim Uhle, News editor of the *Post*, to tell him I wouldn't be at work the next day.

Silvia had not had an easy day. It began about 5:30 A.M. with scrambled eggs and coffee, courtesy city of Louisville. She complained to me later about the quality, but I joked that they apparently had a feast compared to that on the male side of the building. "After breakfast we thought we were going to be able to take it easy, but our naivete was brought to an end right after breakfast when a bunch of us were told we were to scrub

70

floors," she said later. Just as the mopping was to begin, however, she, like all the other demonstrators having only misdemeanor charges, were bailed out with a little of the $20,000 that the Open Housing Committee spent for this purpose within a two-week period.

But out of jail she had no money because it was in her purse, which had been incumbered by police, which meant that it couldn't be gotten until Monday. With no where to go, without a dime of money, and having no friends south of Cincinnati, she started to say yes when asked if she wanted to remain in jail. Then Jackie Price, a black friend she had made in jail, said she could stay at her house.

By the time Jackie and Silvia left jail at 7:00 A.M. and got to her house, Mrs. Price had read Sunday's *Courier-Journal* and told them that there was a story in it about a demonstrator being beaten up and taken to a hospital.

"I was afraid; I didn't know what to do," Silvia said later. Jackie's mother, realizing Silvia's concern, said they knew a minister who would get her to see me. The minister, Episcopal Chaplain at the University of Louisville, got her to the jail at 2:45 that afternoon; but they were told there could be no visitors until the guard was changed an hour later. They waited at a building across the street which the Open Housing Committee used as a rallying point. Someone there told her I'd been beaten up badly, but she relaxed considerably when Hulbert James, a leader of the Louisville demonstrations, assured her that I had been treated at the hospital and that my condition apparently was good because I had refused emergency bail. A less frightened Silvia went back to the jail with Erv Simpson, the minister, to see me after the guard changed. He kept inquiring without success. Silvia became more anxious. They waited. "I was numb with fear," Silvia told me later. "Erv Simpson had spent most of the day trying to find you, and we still couldn't see you. I let him do all the talking. I needed an interpreter. I really felt like I was in a foreign country and was best off letting him talk because he was white."

At 5:00 P.M. jail officials told them I had been taken to the hospital. Reverend Simpson took her there immediately, but at the hospital they were told they couldn't see me because I was in the Emergency Room and a doctor was treating me.

Monday morning Silvia went to court along with dozens of other demonstrators to plead Not Guilty. She described it this way:

I looked and looked for you and couldn't find you, but thought maybe that was just because the court was so jammed with defendants. Then they called the name Patrick Huber and no Patrick Huber was there. My nightmare began all over again. I wanted to run out and look for you, but if I'd done that, they would have sent out a bench warrant for me for not pleading. I figured we didn't need to have two of us in jail.

When she got to the hospital that day, I explained that nothing serious had happened, that the reason I was still there was that when they inserted a needle to feed me insulin and water and glucose intravenously, they had missed the vein in my arm. This meant that the fluid did not get into the blood stream where it was needed. I realized what was wrong and complained, but by the time they took out the needle and reinjected it correctly, the fluid had blown up my forearm to twice its normal size.

"Oh! That sounds bad."

"It's no big problem. I guess you can't expect to have perfect care when you're a prisoner."

"Oh it's good to see you," Silvia said excitedly. "I've been scared to death about you."

I was surprised. I spoke slowly: "You were? I didn't think there was really anything to be bothered about. I wasn't beaten very badly when you stop to think about all the blood thousands of people have shed for civil rights during the last ten years. . . Say. . . did you get a hold of Jim Uhle from the *Post*." She said she had and he said, "Just keep us informed." I said that sounded like him since he was a very understanding person.

"A lot of people have certainly been very helpful to me," she said. "And I talked to one of the attorneys for the demonstrations. And *The New York Times* was here, and he got their reporter to make a statement about what happened."

This interested me more than sympathy. "Was the story in *The New York Times?*" I asked quickly.

"I don't know about that," she replied. "I think this was a statement to defend you in court. The civil rights group here is really well organized. They have worked it out so it doesn't cost anything to be bailed out of jail. The — what do you call them? — have agreed to bail out demonstrators for nothing."

"You mean bondsmen?"

"Yes," she replied.

"That doesn't sound right that they do it for nothing," I challenged her. Actually the Open Housing Committee paid the bail of most demonstrators. Silvia paid mine, however, and was under the illusion that we would get back the $200 check she put up for my $2000 bond.

Tuesday morning I got out of the hospital and appeared in court. After that brief appearance, we started home. Jim Brooks had already taken a bus back to Cincinnati, so it was just the two of us.

On the ride home we visited continuously about the weekend's events. We were both happy — Silvia, mostly because we had "survived"; I, mostly because we had done something that might have positive results. We had not read that morning's *New York Times*, which reported that my beating was one possible reason that so few people showed up for a march Sunday night that it was cancelled.

As we talked about my discomfort, I assumed that she as a black person thought I had done something for her — not something I was obligated to do anyway, but something that had special importance because it was designed to help her people. I thought that's why she enjoyed talking about the whole thing. Seven years later she would tell me that I had little respect for blacks, and that our participation in Louisville was an impractical adventure I undertook for the thrill of it rather than to help black people.

Anyway, we both started learning that weekend that when a biracial couple gets involved with something involving race — anywhere from participation in a racial demonstration to a discussion about the neighborhood block associations's outlook toward integration — there is no biracial couple but rather a black and a white spouse. We would have had to learn this eventually anyway, but the drama of Louisville speeded the learning process. We learned that although we agreed about almost everything we did in Louisville, we were agreeing not as

73

a biracial couple but as one black and one white. We realized that each spouse may criticize his own group, as Silvia did with blacks at the University of Cincinnati and I did with Louisville's white establishment. It would be many years later before we realized that the black spouse is not so free to criticize whites, or the white so free to criticize blacks.

Back in Cincinnati, we drove into our quiet neighborhood, entered our apartment, which was just as it had been left Saturday morning, and stayed there for the evening.

"Don't you want to call your parents?" Silvia asked within a few minutes.

I was unexcited about the idea, saying that if Benedicta called them Sunday morning and Silvia had called them Sunday night, they knew the basic facts.

Monday morning's *Cincinnati Enquirer* ran a three-column UPI picture on the front page of its local news section showing a policeman pinning me to the floor of the police van as blood streamed down my forehead. Their two-column story had emphasized by the second paragraph that I was copy editor for the *Post*, its rival paper, and reported in the following paragraph that my wife was Negro.

This meant that the *Post* that afternoon also had to run a story about it, but they did not identify Silvia as Negro, nor select quite as bloody a picture.

Going to work Wednesday morning, it didn't seem like it was quite the normal day, but close to it. Soon after I began my normal day's work, I was told that the editor wanted to see me. It was obvious what he was going to ask me about, but I was not concerned because I felt that I was in the right and could document that.

The editor was cold, almost icy. He asked me to explain what I had done in Louisville that weekend. Soon he said: "We have a story out there that says you attacked the police."

I replied that I had not, saying I had a story from *The New York Times* supporting what I was saying. Knowing the the *Times* was God in the newspaper world, I was sure that this would convince him. It didn't.

"I don't care what *The New York Times* says. What I want to
74

know is, did you bite the finger of that policeman?"

In another couple minutes I was fired. When I asked why, he said because of incompetence. I realized that was a cover-up, since I had been hired on a six months' trial basis and had been told of no gross incompetence during the five months I had been there. Anyway, he was the boss and I was without a job.

Silvia accepted the firing, at least for the time being, as I accepted it — as further evidence that we were willing to stick out our necks for the cause of racial equality. Indeed, my firing seemed to draw us even closer together. So did our mail.

We felt our Louisville activity was supported by the cards and letters from dozens of friends. But more significant were some unexpected ones. A get well card was sent from the leader of the John Birch Society in the Newark area. Silvia wouldn't admit it, but this showed me that people can be very kind despite their adhering to what seems to be harsh political dogma.

The official board of my hometown church wrote a letter of support to us. Also unexpected was a card from staff members of *The Newark Advocate*. Even more unexpected was a letter from a Clarksville widow whom Silvia had seen only once, and I had never known very well. She, like my aunt in another letter, quoted Scripture as encouragement.

The only grim letters came from my parents, mostly from my father. When I talked to my father Wednesday night, he was very upset, seeming to think I was going to serve the maximum sentence of some eight or ten years, for which I could be committed if found guilty on all seven charges. The letter he wrote Sunday was messy and showed concern, but was rational. The next several were not. Wednesday's said: "Mother. . . told me not to think but to keep active. I have failed in both ventures. I am now thinking at random or worse. Mother and I would like to help you, and scold you, Pat. The scolding has been done by the law. I am a clubhouse lawyer, so much of the advice I write is useless. But here goes, assuming your mail is not bugged." By Thursday's letter his printing was almost illegible, he was calling the policeman pictured holding me on the van floor as a "thirty-year-late Hitler youth culprit who is not only a right-wing Klansman, but a schizophrenic psycho-

75

pathic with a severe delusion of grandeur." He sent a $500 check, the first of several, to institute a $500,000 damage suit against the Louisville Police force.

I was amazed. I wrote him a letter stating that my health was fine, that I thought there was at least some moral basis for participating in the march, and that there was no reason for concern legally since the charges were trumped up and my lawyer was qualified and white.

My parents' concern proved that Silvia was wise in calling them Sunday and in urging me to do so once I got out of the hospital. It showed how wrong I was when, although I did not say so, I regarded her calls to Benedicta and my parents as unsophisticated black or Spanish emotionalism

Within the week I recognized that my parents were concerned, as are thousands of middle class parents each year, when they learn that their "well bred" youngsters have been arrested in a demonstration. I did not appreciate until recently, however, that this event was different from most because it was not just a son and wife arrested in a peace march, nor a son arrested with white, or even black friends, in a civil rights march. This was a white son arrested with his black wife in a march for integrated housing. I now realize it would be difficult for either of our parents to think of our interracial activities in Louisville, without thinking also about our interracial marriage.

My parents never mentioned or implied that my involvement was related to my wife's being black. They knew I had been the instigator, and they expressed concern about Silvia, not blame toward her. I now suspect, however, that consciously or subconsciously it increased their anxiety about our interracial marriage.

For the moment — and this would change six or seven years later —the anxiety of my parents made me feel further from them and closer to Silvia. The letters and phone calls from friends made us feel very close because they involved something we had done together for the same purpose and because of the same philosophy. For years we would be brought closer together merely by visiting with each other and friends about that wild weekend. The challenges, such as my having to get a new job and our having to move and our having to pay legal expenses, would unite us even more. It had an effect something like that experienced during World War II when the challenge of the outside oppressor caused certain national groups to forget about many of their differences with their fellow countrymen. Often a couple facing challenges experiences the same phenomenon, but it seemed particularly easy for us to regard our challenges positively because they were the product of a demonstration based on the philosophy that blacks and whites could associate with each other, the very conviction upon which our marriage was founded.

We felt very close. We also had gained recognition of the difficulty of correcting momentous social problems. We agreed with each other within a few days that we had gotten an increased understanding of why so many adults concern themselves with such non-monumental issues as neighborhoods, relatives, and children. We decided that if we were to retreat momentarily from the problems of the nation, we would need a problem on the family level to challenge us.

Thus an event inspired by our desire to make the world in our own image led several weeks later to the conception of someone in our own image.

CHAPTER V

A Long Shot

The foreman in the job printing shop in Brooklyn had been very helpful, but there are always problems on that first night of publication. Silvia had waited patiently most of the evening, helping me in whatever way she could; but we finally had a little argument, and she went out to the car with her mother, her two nephews, and Heather, our three-month-old daughter.

About 9:00 P.M. the first page proofs were made and as I showed them to Silvia she exclaimed with joy: "Oh Pat! That looks so good." Still surprised, she added after looking at them a few moments: "I never thought it would look like that. That looks like a professional job."

It was a professional job. She was talking about the first issue of *The Fort Greene Observer*, a four-page tabloid community newspaper we were starting to publish for the Fort Greene area of Brooklyn, the section where Silvia's sister still lived, and near where we'd been married.

It was Wednesday, and the issue was dated for the next day, April 11, 1968. That's why the two lead stories and picture on the front page involved the assassination of the Reverend Dr. Martin Luther King, Jr, nine days earlier. On page 2, underneath an editorial about Dr. King, was one explaining the purpose of the paper. Silvia said she liked the way I'd written that many persons had asked our motives, and had asked what political faction, ethnic group, or business or labor group we represented. "One sounds both dishonest and naive to say he is attempting to publish a newspaper that writes fairly about the entire community, not just a particular part of it," I wrote.

"Naive or not, however, a newspaper for this area has to be our explanation because it is our goal.

"Some have said a newspaper in this area won't work. Their arguments are strengthened by the bilingual nature of the community, the large number living inside the area but working outside it, and many other factors.

"We think, however, the area can make good use of a good newspaper. That is why we are going to try to make it good and hope you use it."

We had been in Fort Greene about two months so that I could plan the publication of the paper. I'd suggested the venture after my mediocre copy editing caused a daily in Harrisburg, Pennsylvania, to dismiss me in February, a month after our first youngster was born.

Since the Louisville affair we had been busy moving from Cincinnati, adjusting to a new area, dealing with my being hospitalized briefly, and looking forward to the birth of our first youngster. Our business with these conventional things overshadowed the fact we were biracial. The only way our biracialness affected us was that it made us particularly happy to be expectant parents: we were certain that we would be good parents, and that our happy biracial child would further document the success of our biracial marriage.

As was the case in Louisville, I was the instigator of this venture in idealism. This extensive degree of racial involvement is not experienced by most biracial couples and it was the last of it for us, but these two extraordinary activities illustrate a phenomena that continued to occur during ordinary times of our marriage, and that probably occurs in many biracial marriages. The phenomena is a pressure I felt to respond to racial injustice more intensely than I would if not married to a black. And even if my black spouse cared little about racial problems, I could not be disinterested until I looked at my marital relationship, not just my conscience.

Besides the pressure, having a black wife made it a lot more feasible to publish in a ghetto, particularly when she was Spanish and the ghetto was one-third Spanish. I was interested in any ghetto, but Silvia and I agreed that Fort Greene would be the best bet because her sister still lived there and might get a few friends to buy the paper. Benedicta would also be able to educate us about the neighborhood.

I decided that the project was worth $1500 or $2000 of my savings — I didn't really consider them *our* savings. I knew the odds were against the success of the paper, but I thought the community benefit that would result if it succeeded made it worth the "long shot." During my first week in Fort Greene, while explaining my plans to a priest, Father Sullivan walked toward us. He said he was pessimistic about the chances for success. I was sorry about the pessimism, but felt good about seeing the man who had married. us. It made me proud that Silvia and I were not only a biracial couple that had stayed happily married, but that we had not turned our back on the ghetto and were returning to it to try to be constructive.

As soon as Silvia and I told her about the paper, Benedicta arranged to have us share, rent free, an office on Myrtle Avenue being used by a Puerto Rican group. The location was ideal, just a few blocks from the huge low income public housing project and the slums surrounding it. This part of Myrtle Avenue, decorated by the ugly steel and concrete of an elevated train track, was the commercial center for Fort Greene, lined with many small stores secure from vandalism only because of the steel fences their owner-operators locked in front of their windows at the close of each business day.

Driving limitation and philosophical orientation made me want to live within the area to be served. Ineligible for the low income public housing and unexcited about a couple of tenements where I sought to rent an apartment, I took the advice of a drunk who pointed out an apartment "that was very nice although they'll want a high price for it." The apartment was not extravagant — in fact, my mother described it years later as an extremely depressing place, but it was adequate and low priced.

I had almost always rented our apartments for us, not out of design but because of convenience. Landlords may have been surprised when they saw my wife, but nothing happened. This time something did. Since the apartment was empty, we moved in that night, or rather tried to move in. After Silvia drove our car full of belongings from Benedicta's apartment, where we'd been staying, her two nephews ran up to the apartment with me and started helping me unload. By the second or third trip, I was met by a very concerned Albert Vitti, who owned the second floor apartment I had rented, along with the first floor apartment where he lived with his wife and two daughters.

He raised his hand, urging me to come toward him. "I can't rent this apartment to you." Then a pause. "I hadn't had a chance to tell my wife about this before she saw you, but I can't rent it because it is tied up in an estate."

I looked at him a moment. He looked at me a moment. We knew that wasn't the reason he refused to rent. Finally, when he continued to refuse, I called the police to get the matter on record.

The next morning Silvia, Benedicta, and I started taking Mrs. Vitti's handwritten receipt to me around to various governmental agencies seeking to get admittance; but learned that New York's housing discrimination law did not apply to two-family residences. Finally I called up the lawyer I had gotten to represent our newspaper, and he went to work. Within two days he had gotten Vitti's attorney to agree not only to refund our deposit but to pay us other compensation which would more than pay for our legal costs. The deal was good, and so I told our attorney to proceed.

Happy we had obtained a settlement so favorable and obtained it so quickly, I called Silvia to tell her the good news. She surprised me. She shocked me.

"You agreed to give up the apartment? Why did you do that? I want to make them let us in."

"But the deal is very favorable to us," I tried to explain.

"I don't care how much money we get out of it, I don't want to make a settlement unless they agree to rent it to us," she snapped back.

"Well I've already told the lawyer to go ahead and make the settlement," I explained.

"I don't care. Call him up and tell him we want in the apartment."

I suggested she think the matter over a little bit and weigh
81

the advantage of the proposed settlement before we do anything more. I told her I'd call her back in an hour.

She called me back at the newspaper office in forty-five minutes, even more adamant than before. It seemed such a reversal of our usual roles — Pat being the advocate of moderation and practicality and expediency, and Silvia ready to defend principal and honor at any cost.

I felt embarassed as I called the lawyer to ask him to reject the settlement I had told him two hours earlier to accept. He was angry. He emphasized the benefits of the settlement he had worked out. "If I go back to their lawyer now, this is going to mean more bargaining, and it is going to mean his fee will be increased and my fee will increase. I've gotten you the best possible deal."

"I know you have. You did a good job and it is only fair that we should pay you for any additional time you spend. All I can say is that my wife has become very emotionally involved in this. Even though usually she is very calm about such things, for some reason she will agree to nothing but a greater effort to make them rent the apartment to us. That's all I can say to you."

Within a few days the attorney had gotten the Vitti's to let us move into the apartment, which we did quickly. Soon after going to bed that first night, we visited briefly about having come out on top in our first confrontation with housing discrimination. It was no big victory as far as I was concerned, however, because had we not moved there, we could have lived somewhere nearby. I did not fully appreciate my black spouse's emotional reaction to being told she could not rent because of the color of her skin. I understood better than she the sentiments of the Vitti's. This was made easier later that evening as yelling and bottle-breaking and some small explosions continued long past midnight. Silvia told me she was afraid, and I said this opened my mind to the fear the Vitti's had of renting to a black, since most of the hell outside their windows was being raised by blacks. Any black, any middle class white liberal, any social worker, any college professor, can determine with ease that Silvia's two nephews starting to move

82

n our furniture would not necessarily behave like the young ruffians in the street, just because they were the same color; but that recognition is not so easy to make when you are in the middle of the real thing.

By the time we were ready to publish that first edition, we had both learned a lot about Fort Greene and something about our relationship with each other. This was my first direct exposure to the ghetto life in which Silvia had grown up. I had visited her there, had talked at length with her about her teenage environment and the significance of the way it differed from mine, and had gotten married there, — but all that had been but an introduction. It was not until I lived in the ghetto that I comprehended the full significance of the difference between our backgrounds. And Fort Greene taught Silvia something similar. It had been easy to move from a ghetto to become a middle class wife. It wasn't until she moved back to the ghetto with me that she fully recognized the significance of having left it in the first place. Every "poor black become middle class" must relate the goals and principles of his old ghetto culture to those of the middle class environment; but this is easier when you are making the reassessment with a black spouse, rather than one of another culture. Silvia had already told me her disgust about certain activities of blacks and Puerto Ricans, but rather than a black sharing her disappointment with her fellow black spouse, she was having to analyze it for her white spouse. And when she saw economic injustices perpetrated by the white establishment, it would have been easy to express her anger with a black spouse, but it was not quite so easy to be a black spouse expressing anti-white sentiments to her white husband, even though he might agree completely.

After the page proofs had been made and corrected, and final proofs had been printed for offset photographing that night, it was about 10:00 o'clock. Silvia left Heather with Benedicta, and we happily headed for the firm's offset press plant on Long Island. We weren't holding hands, we may even have been on opposite sides of the car, but we couldn't have been closer as we rode to the plant. The firm's employees were very helpful: we wondered if maybe their cooperativeness and the very favorable rate their boss gave us might have been an endorsement for the sort of thing this couple — this biracial couple — was doing.

After the offset plates had been made and the ultra-modern press began to roll around 11:30 P.M., I grabbed up several of the first copies.

"No! Don't take those. Those aren't any good," said the plant manager as his two pressmen adjusted the press.

"I know these are rejects," I said, "but I wanted to get them so we will have something to show our grandchildren."

His accomodating Jewish nature came forth strong as he smiled and said: "Don't worry. We will get you some extra ones for that once the press is adjusted."

The printer had agreed to print 4000 copies of the first two issues and use extra-good stock for them, both of which were to be giveaways. Silvia did not realize how much work it is to give away 4000 newspapers; and I did not realize that she did not expect to do most of the work. Anyway, most of them were distributed; and I was back on the sidewalk Friday morning selling advertising for the second issue. On most issues I spent fifty hours of my eighty-hour week trying to sell advertising; for the second issue I spent even more than that, realizing that the paper could not survive without advertising.

Our life was built around the paper. After spending most of the day selling advertising, there was usually a community meeting of some sort to attend at night, either for a story or to gain identity in the community. Often Silvia went with me; and this seemed natural since she was the Spanish and black half of the paper. Going to the meetings, like going to most discussions of racial and social problems, made us feel closer together. The discussion at home after the meetings made us feel even closer. We almost always agreed when residents were justified in condemning the white establishment and when the residents themselves created the problems. Our agreement proved to us that neither of us looked at people as blacks or whites, but rather as human beings. After all, we knew that was the way we looked at each other.

Our feeling of closeness became particularly great on Wednesday afternoon as the deadline approached. Any couple pro-

84

bably becomes closer when working cooperatively to publish their paper, run their little grocery store, or whatever; but we weren't just a couple — we were a black and white couple doing something together in an area that seemed to say loudly that blacks and whites could not work together. This was a little extra tie between us when the shop foreman complimented me on my page layouts, when the local school principal gave us her compliments, etc. And the cooperation between this black woman and white man was symbolized in a far corner of that print shop, unnoticed by printers and even by father. Heather, hungry like most four-month-old babies, would get her milk from the breast of her mother as she waited to take us to the offset plant.

The lead story in the third edition told something of the area. It was about an active community leader, a brother to the chairman of Mayor John Lindsay's Urban Task Force for Fort Greene, who had been found dead in the street ten blocks from our apartment, apparently murdered in the predawn hours.

We had a problem that was trivial compared to that. As had been planned, the paper went on sale for ten cents starting with this issue, and the press run was cut to 2000. That afternoon three boys selling the paper on Myrtle Avenue ran back into the office, chased by a gang of boys trying to take money and papers from them. I went out on the sidewalk, despite Silvia's advice, to protest to the boys. Suddenly I was attacked by fifteen or twenty of them, all under age thirteen or fourteen.

"Call the police," Silvia yelled as they threw me to the sidewalk and jumped on me. Silvia fainted and was carried inside the office, where by then some of the young ruffians had gone in and banged on our typewriter, took copies of the paper, and started fighting with one of the three boys chased into the office in the first place. By the time two policemen appeared, adults in the area had gotten the boys off me, and I suffered no serious injury. Of course my watch was gone by then. I told the policeman this and pointed out five or six of the boys who had led the attack on me, suggesting they search them to try to find the watch.

"Don't worry. If we find a watch, we'll tell you about it and let you identify it," one of the policemen responded blandly.

Seeing that no one had been seriously injured, the police ended their investigation. As I watched the two white men of the law walk away routinely from the fifteen or twenty black ruffians, I realized that I had had the experience of having had my rights ignored because I was white. Silvia agreed. This injustice was easier to bear because when we went home that night, I could receive sympathy from a wife that was black. As we talked about the incident and about the three boys — all black — afraid to go back into the street to sell the paper, we agreed that next time before we automatically sided with those attacking police brutality in black neighborhoods, we would remember it is also possible to have too little authority from police. In fact that is what I said in an editorial the next week.

The attack by the gang, along with other developments, convinced me all the more of the importance of a good newspaper in Fort Greene, so I worked all the harder trying to sell ads for the next issue, as well as getting good news copy. Wednesday night was even later than usual; and the early-morning ride back from Long Island did not have the romance of the one following the first edition. I was exhausted Thursday morning. I would liked to have slept until 9 A.M., but I pushed myself into getting up so I could get some papers sold. When Silvia told me she was not going to get out of bed and deliver some papers, I blew up in frustration and slapped her, telling her my whole week's work would be lost if we didn't get the papers circulated.

She yelled at me, jumped out of bed, and told me how mean it was for me to hit her. I was completely surprised by the length and emotionalness of her complaint. Although I knew no woman — or man — enjoys being hit, I didn't realize that a Spanish woman regards it as a particularly brutal insult. I tried to explain my concern about getting the paper delivered, but she paid no attention, repeating her condemnation of my striking her. She told me she didn't care about getting the paper out — she was too upset by my having hit her. Consequently I left the apartment right after breakfast to get to work as quickly as possible on the distribution job.

86

As I started selling them, I didn't understand why she wasn't more enthusiastic about distributing the papers. She said she was tired. Well, I sure in the hell was tired too, but I wasn't going to let that stop me. I thought she was an ambitious person — working her way through college and all that — how come she wasn't willing to push a little longer with this paper? I certainly had pushed myself, physically and emotionally; and all I wanted was for her to do the same. As I'd told her before, I'd never forget my hardworking paternal grandfather telling me: "If anything is worth doing, it is worth doing well." I thought she went along with that, but maybe not — maybe she was more like those blacks and Spanish in Fort Greene whose biggest problem was that they wouldn't work hard enough with something and stick with it long enough to make it a success.

About 11 A.M., realizing that Silvia would have calmed down, put my slap into perspective, and recognized the importance of getting the paper into the hands of readers, I called her at home to ask when she'd be able to start helping me.

"I'm not going to help you! " she shot back. "I told you I won't stand for your striking me."

"Oh come on. Don't make a big deal out of a little thing. We've got to get these papers out."

"It's not a little thing. I called your parents up about it, and they're very upset too. They're going to come and see us tomorrow."

Stunned. Unbelieving. Heartbroken. Angry was I. Silvia had indeed lost touch with reality. Here we were arguing about selling a few papers for ten cents a piece, and she gets my parents to spend $250 on plane tickets to come and mediate the dispute.

I immediately walked to our apartment, called my parents, and talked to my mother, who expressed amazement at this brutal wife-beating devil into which her son had turned.

"I just can't imagine you doing anything like that," she said accusingly.

"You've got to realize this is a very drab world here in the ghetto, and it's not always as easy to stay calm and friendly as it is in Clarksville, Iowa."

"That doesn't have anything to do with it," my non-understanding mother threw back at me, rejecting my suggestion they not come.

As my parents flew into John F. Kennedy Airport Friday morning, I was extremely frustrated. I was frustrated enough to let race cast a negative influence in my marriage for the first time in the five years I had known Silvia. I didn't have any doubts about the strength of our marriage — in fact I knew that *The Fort Greene Observer* had brought us even closer together than we had been. My racial thoughts had to do with my parents and how they would relate this crisis they believed existed to the fact that we were a biracial couple. Was this a crisis they had expected since three years ago when they had come to this "foreign" neighborhood to go to a church of a "foreign" religion to see us married? Would they wonder what kind of ruffian they had produced or this inner-city ghetto had produced? The questions and fears were simple ones — questions and fears that could be taken care of through communication with my parents. But when my parents arrived, said hello, and came to our apartment, I did not feel free to communicate with them, at least about the race business. The breakdown in communication was particularly significant because my parents and I had always felt so free to talk with each other, no matter what the subject.

As my mother started questioning me, I wondered if mother and dad were really that shocked by my actions, or if consciously or subconsciously they felt obliged to show that as in-laws to a person of another color, they were out to protect her. My suspicion of this increased when after Silvia started out by saying that in her culture it was considered very brutal for men to hit their wives, my mother replied quickly: "We did not bring Pat up with the idea that a man can hit his wife. He was taught to know better."

The big issue was not race, of course — it was just that the racial differences threatened to cloud the real issues. By Saturday morning, Mom and Dad had had an opportunity to get acquainted with their new and only grandchild — this was the last time Dad would see her, Silvia had relaxed a little, I had

88

been condemned by everybody for hitting my wife, and my parents had heard enough about the newspaper to encourage me to work a little less hard and not feel ashamed of myself if it did not succeed.

Whereas I, the young adventuresome member of the family, had had some difficulty in adjusting to Fort Greene, to my parents it was an area impossible to comprehend — or trust.

"How come all those kids aren't in school," my dad said to me as we walked from our apartment to the newspaper office about 10:30 A.M. Realizing he was uneasy, and suspecting he thought there was a mass wave of truancy, I thought a moment searching for an explanation, smiled, and said: "Because this is Saturday."

"Oh that's right — I wasn't thinking about that," he said as he smiled back.

There were other things in Fort Greene dad couldn't laugh about. But there was a sense of identity in that regardless of the practicality of my enterprise, I was something like the small-town businessman just starting out and bothered by the lack of revenue. Seeing my concern, he helped the *Observer* out $7 or $8, and helped both our spirits a lot more than that by selling a column advertisement to the corner drugstore for next week's issue. "He really got a thrill out of selling that ad," mom told me later.

After they had gone home, I said to Silvia: "I was trying to figure out what my dad's reaction was about having a son publishing a paper in a place like this."

"I think he respects you for doing something like this, but yet is glad he isn't doing it," she responded.

And as Silvia said this, I felt that she admired me too: that was the big thing my parents' visit had shown. I needed some of Silvia's thoughts put in my parents' mouths so that they sounded consistent with my upbringing. She needed some of my actions and thoughts reflected in my parents, so she could better understand the problem as well as the cure. She needed to know, for example, that Huber could not tolerate defeat when he went on a business venture: that didn't justify his beating his wife, but it did inevitably frustrate him. And I needed to hear my mother

say that Silvia couldn't spend much of her time on the *Observe*
because she had a four-month old daughter to take care o
Silvia had said that, but I had wondered if maybe she wasn'
like most of those Catholics — particularly the Spanish ones -
attaching a little too much importance to raising babies. Bu
when my middle class, one-child Presbyterian mother said it
then it must be true.

And in spite of the few days of friction, the *Observer* ha
brought us closer together because we were committed to it
purpose and wanted to use our biracialness to make it succeed
In Louisville agreement on the objective had brought ou
biracial selves close together throughout the whole thing be
cause the issue was simple and the time short. With Fort Greene
overall agreement on the goals did not mean we were alway
being drawn closer together, because here our endeavor wa
relatively long, the issues complex, and the problems many. So
as we later saw many times, when our relationship went well
our biracialness made it just a little bit better, and when ou
relationship went bad, our biracialness made it just a little bi
worse.

For the most part, our Fort Greene relationship was good
even though advertising and circulation were not. I was bacl
that Monday morning trying to use my white face to convinc
white businessmen that the *Observer* was run with white know
how and yet identified with the local residents. Silvia was bacl
the next Thursday delivering the paper to apartments in th
area. Within a few weeks, her load was getting a little heavier -
not with the newspapers but with growing Heather, whom sh
carried on her back. One of our new subscribers was easy t
reach, Mr. and Mrs. Vitti. It gave me increased confidence i
mankind when we had lived a month in their apartment (an
our legal right to live there had expired), and they not only ha
become communicative to us, but also had the subscriptio
price of the paper deducted from our second month's rent.
didn't understand why Silvia was more hesitant to praise them
but then I overlooked the probability that in her mind th
initial rejection had not been to us, but to her.

Starting May 23, the seventh issue, I tried to make up for ou
90

ow circulation by cutting the price to five cents and by also
aving the paper sold on thirty commercial newsstands through-
ut the area. About 3 P.M. that Wednesday, Silvia happened to
e with me as I got a story. Five hours later, when she saw the
tory on page one, she said proudly: "Pat! That's just the way
: happened. I didn't realize there was a story there."

She used two of her talents about this time too — her per-
onality and her linguistic ability — to sell a couple of adver-
isements to Spanish businesses. "I'm going to sell them another
d next week," she explained. "They sell a lot of trinkets and
eligious statues and Spanish people like that junk."

This made us feel close to each other — the fact we were both
ising our talents and our diverse cultures to make this thing a
uccess. The one facet I missed is that although it was perfectly
ermissible for her to speak derogatorily about her ethnic
roup, it would not be the same when her white husband did it.
'd learn that five years later, just like she'd learn that although
 considered it fine when I criticized the WASP culture of small
own America, I would be angered when she did the same thing.

The next month we worked hard, stayed close to each other,
nd the paper went on with advertising revenue just great
nough to cover printing costs. More depressing than the paper's
roblems were the community's problems. Our pessimism was
oint and directed against everybody — whites and blacks, rich
nd poor. That's why we endured it much better than we would
ave been able to do had we both been black, or both been
vhite.

The community's problems weren't helped by the local War
n Poverty agency or by politics. I got my first, firsthand intro-
luction to big city political pressures on June 12, when a
epresentative of Congressman John Rooney stuffed $200 cash
n my hand and told me to run a page advertisement. When I
sked the young Rooney representative what to put in the ad.,
e replied: "I don't care what you put in it. Just find any-
hing." When I explained that he had given me $40 more than
he charge for a one-page ad., he said: "Oh just keep it. That's
ll right."

I couldn't help but think how much "generosity money"

91

must go to other people of influence when so much was given to a low circulation paper that had just been started. But it had done its job. Peter Eikenberry, a young idealistic lawyer who lived in the neighborhood and was a personal friend of ours, was the Liberal Party candidate for the Democratic nomination for Congress and the best man for the job, but I couldn't help him.

And Silvia's and my pessimism about Fort Greene resulted from the shortcomings of local residents as well as those of outsiders. This was reflected in my June 13 editorial, based on Edward Kennedy's eulogy in St. Patrick's Cathedral the Saturday before, for his assassinated brother. The editorial was based on Robert Kennedy's statement: "Some men see things as they are and ask why, I dream things that never were and ask why not?"

"Certainly there is a need," the editorial said, "to look at things as they are and ask why. . . Fort Greene has reached the point where it needs a lot fewer whys and a lot more why nots. . . Some people look at unfortunate parts of Fort Greene and say nothing. Some say why are things like they are and encourage us to cry about our problems. The great need is for those who 'dream things that never were and say why not?' "

And there were people in Fort Greene asking why not; and Silvia and I both appreciated them and so they brought us closer together. And they were all types of people and all colors of peoples, and so it brought us even closer together to know that some of these people sincerely dedicated in helping the downtrodden were Silvia's color and some were my color. There was Marvin Parks, whose skill and dedication in working with puppets, some of it under a War on Poverty program, inspired children enough to justify overlooking ten War on Poverty programs that didn't work. There was Dr. Stanley Bergen (who later became my personal physician), who believed medicine was to help human beings rather than a device for getting rich, and consequently worked late many nights trying to establish a public health program in Fort Greene. And there was Terri Bush, an energetic young consultant to the City's Department of Cultural Affairs: when she told us about her plans for Voice of the Children, a writing workshop for neighborhood youngsters,

92

we thought her intentions good and published a story about her, but thought she was a dreamer. She was a dreamer. That's why the Voice of the Children developed, as evidenced two years later in the publication of a book consisting of poems and short essays from twenty-six ghetto teenagers.

From the time we moved to Fort Greene until the time we left, I felt closer to Silvia's relatives than I have felt at any other time. Once I lived in the ghetto, I understood them better than I had, and I felt that they were more open to me. The significance of this is that since we, like most biracial couples, have not lived in the same type environment as the black partner's relatives, it was hard to get to feel close to them, and continue feeling close to them.

One of the ironies of Fort Greene involved Cecilia and me on the afternoon of June 6. Our ninth edition, published that day, had a lead story about public meetings that night regarding how some $200,000 in federal anti-poverty funds were to be distributed in the area. Beneath it was a picture and a two-column story about a group, called the N.U.T.S., which had attacked the local anti-poverty office a week earlier and thrown a chair through a glass partition. The group was angered about their request for some $25,000 in federal funds, supposedly to be used for narcotics prevention. Some local residents said it was for narcotics purchase. A lengthy editorial, titled "NUTS to N.U.T.S.", urged residents to deny funds to them, thus making more money available for other community projects.

That afternoon the president and four or five members of N.U.T.S. came to the *Observer* office to protest the editorial and story. Soon the president charged: "I think you're prejudiced. Tell me, are you prejudiced?"

I leaned back in my chair and spoke as if I were a college philosophy professor. "I think all people are probably prejudiced in one way or another. Yes. I'd say I'm prejudiced in some ways."

My chair was over before the sentence was finished, and I was on the floor. They made quick work of me. As they stopped, Cecilia came in the door, ran over to me on the floor, bent down and yelled: "Oh my God." And so with my black mother-in-law bending over her "prejudiced" son-in-law, the N.U.T.S decided to leave.

An incident like this was not going to stop me, but the lack of progress through June 20 encouraged Silvia and me to call it quits. Starting the paper had been easier because we were bi-racial; stopping the paper was easier for the same reason because it was not two blacks deserting their own people or two whites merely thinking they had done as much as they should. Instead it was one black and one white realizing that there was no point in publishing beyond June 27.

So I was an unemployed newspaperman in the city of New York in mid-1968. That meant I had better leave newspapering or leave New York, because there were too many veteran newsmen from the demised *New York Herald Tribune* and *The New York World Telegram and Sun* to provide much of an opportunity for a relatively inexperienced person like myself. Silvia wanted to stay with her family and I didn't mind that. So trade journalism was the next alternative to newspapering. I got a job with *Corset Bra and Lingerie Magazine*. Writing about bras is not stimulating — intellectually or otherwise — but it was a relief to have a worry-free job and a regular paycheck. And we weren't leaving Fort Greene, so it was an interesting contrast to my Manhattan job.

In late November, 1968, Silvia and I decided it would be helpful if she would visit a mutual friend who had suffered an emotional breakdown, so she and Heather flew to our friend's home 400 miles away. When the phone rang about 7:30 A.M. December 4, I wondered why she would be calling.

"Hello. Pat? How are you this morning." I recognized my mother's voice. "Are Silvia and Heather all right?"

"Yes," I responded. "They are with a friend of ours. How come you are calling this time of day."

"I called to tell you your father passed away early this morning," she said calmly.

Disappointed but not upset, I calmly asked the details, told her when I'd leave for Iowa, and told her I'd get in touch with Silvia. That was my mother's and my matter of fact way of dealing with life — and death. Silvia couldn't understand my

94

ack of emotion when I called her a few minutes later. She was the one to express the sorrow, even though it was my father, a man I much admired and one whom she always considered cold. That shows how cold and disinterested in her family I must have seemed to Silvia three months earlier, when she called me up at work crying, telling me that her niece Sandra, the flower girl at our wedding, had leukemia. I showed no emotion over the phone, stating merely that I was sorry to hear about it and wondered if there was anything possible to do to save her life. At the funeral a week later, I'm sure my Spanish wife, if not my black wife, wished I'd shown at least a little emotion, even though she knew I didn't get emotional about such things.

Sometime in early 1969 Silvia got a call from me about a very different sort of matter.

"I can't believe this," she told me over the phone. "Patrick — where did you say you were? Are you serious?"

I chuckled into the pay phone in the lobby of a Forty Second Street striptease house. "Things were disgusting in Louisville, so I thought I'd get a little distraction. I just wanted to let you know where I was and what I was doing."

"How come you are telling me?" she giggled.

After a few more minutes of entertaining conversation, I said I'd have to leave to get back for the second act. "I don't want to miss any, since this is the first one I've ever seen. I'll tell you about Louisville when I get home in two or three hours."

I'd gone to Louisville expecting a trial, since an earlier trip had resulted in a postponement to this date. Instead my $100 plane ticket and loss of a day's pay had netted me another postponement, with the prosecution saying it was not convenient for one of its witnesses, a policeman, to testify because he was off duty that day. The judge criticized the police, pointing out that I had come a long way for the trial, but he postponed my case again.

Done early, I took home the next flight, which happened to be to Newark. That's how I ended up on Forty Second Street.

That night the sense of unity Silvia and I got at Louisville appeared again as we discussed the judicial trickery of the prosecution. By this time the Supreme Court had declared unconstitutional three of the charges against the Louisville demonstrators, including the two against Silvia and three of those against me. A couple more against me had been dropped, but the felony charge remained; and rather than play the flying game between New York and Louisville, I eventually had my lawyer settle the matter out of court.

During 1969 our marriage benefited from a couple of weekend ski trips — a new adventure for both of us — and a vacation in Puerto Rico. In Puerto Rico, Silvia, of course, did all the communicating with the natives and told me all about the island. I'm not sure whether this meant I respected her and enjoyed receiving the fruits of a bicultural relationship, or whether it meant that I lowered her to the position of a tour guide; but in any event it was an enjoyable trip.

Our next trip was south. I never had intended to stay in trade journalism indefinitely, even though I was happy at *Corset Bra and Lingerie Magazine* and had received a modest raise. When offered a job as a copy editor on *The Miami News*, I was delighted about the opportunity to get back into newspapering. Silvia was happy, I was delighted. My chief concern was heat, since I never liked warm weather. Silvia also was concerned about moving South — not because of the weather but because she feared racial heat. Thus when we both crossed the Mason-Dixon line for the first time in September, 1969, we wondered what we would find as we went onward South.

CHAPTER VI

Onward South

The husky fifty-year-old owner of the six-family apartment complex moved his hand to tell me to come to the corner of the living room in which he stood. "I want to talk to you, Mr. Huber. Come on in here," he said as he gestured toward the nearby bathroom. After I obliged him and he closed the door behind us while Silvia continued to move things into the living room, he looked at me, face wrinkled, almost grim, and said softly yet challengingly: "Why didn't you tell me your wife was black?"

Knowing that subject had to be the purpose of his beckoning me to the 4' by 6' room, I was neither surprised nor bothered.

"You never asked me what color she was," I said innocently. "I didn't think that was of any significance."

"There aren't any blacks living around here. This is a very peaceful neighborhood and the people living here want it that way. . . I'll give you your deposit check back and you can move your things out."

I was very low-key, telling him that our brief meeting with one or two of the neighbors did not indicate there would be any problem. When he said he'd contact his lawyer, I reminded him of the obvious: I had a receipt he had given me a day earlier for a deposit and one month's rent.

The landlord remained as Silvia and I prepared to move our furniture into the apartment from the front yard where it had been unloaded by a couple of friends from *The Miami News*, after they had moved it from a warehouse where it had been in storage. Silvia quickly went to a nearby store and bought every

97

kind of cleanser and other cleaning agent she could find, and so together we proceeded to scrub the floors along with most every other part of the house. We really were not that interested in having a house quite *that* clean, but recognized that as the landlord stared at us, we might wash away a little of the stereotype of blacks being dirty. Whether this helped or not, we did not hear anything from the landlord until it was almost time for our second month's rent; and he was then more interested in having our check in his account than in having us out of his apartment. Our relationship with him gradually became more personal and friendly, and there was no problem between us during the two years we lived there.

The morning after we moved in, I recalled the incident to my boss at the *News*. He responded by smiling and paraphrasing the words of the first United States astronaut on the moon: "One small step for mankind." He had gone with me to the apartment the day I rented it, partly because Silvia was sick and I needed a ride, and partly because her giving me the ride even if she were in good health might decrease our chances of renting it. We both enjoyed telling this incident to our friends later, regarding it as an amusing and possibly productive action we took which we could not have taken had we both been black, or both white.

Other than the housing business, race was no significant factor during our first months in Miami. On our trip moving from New York to Miami, Silvia was a little bothered by her stereotype of the South once we got into the Carolinas and Georgia, but nothing happened. When we went to supper together at a nice small-town Georgia restaurant, she didn't laugh at my joke that they might nail us to a cross after we sat down together, but after the meal we agreed that even though the waitress seemed a little surprised, her primary concern soon became our tip rather than our color. We felt close together on the trip, mostly because this was our first long trip with Heather, and because we were heading toward a new place where we would be living together. I thought that whatever concern Silvia did have about the racial attitudes of Southerners was based on the simple fact that she was black; but she explained to me later that her concern was that she was a black traveling with a white.

98

She needed reassurance, I provided it, and this also made us feel closer together.

As we approached Miami, we delighted in seeing for the first time the big blue sky for which the city is famous. As we agreed, its beauty was at least as great as represented in the pictures we'd seen. I forgot that this was September and that the weather got hotter in the summer, not cooler.

After several unsuccessful calls to try to rent an apartment, we obtained temporary residence for the night in a motel. We ended up living in this "temporary" residence two weeks. Our problem was not Silvia's color, it was having a youngster, which excluded us from most apartments being rented. Besides that, relatively few apartments were being rented because of Miami's housing shortage at that time due to the mass influx of Cubans.

After two weeks of living in our motel — paying at the daily rate — and still unable to find an unfurnished apartment, I became desparate enough to rent a furnished one even though our furniture was on the way from New York. In another two weeks, after the furniture had arrived and had been put in a warehouse, we decided we had to find an unfurnished apartment. When I went to the landlord to ask if we could cancel our one-year lease, I made sure Silvia went along and met him for the first time. Upon being introduced to her, he listened sympathetically to our problem of not wanting to pay high storage costs for our furniture and having to use the older furniture with which his apartment was furnished. He not only offered to release us from the lease without penalty, but gave us back the half of the month's rent we had paid but not yet used. Silvia and I joked afterwards about whether he did this because he was a nice guy or because he was shocked at seeing the other half of the couple to whom he had granted the lease.

I enjoyed my work at the *News*, particularly because I liked so many people on its staff, even though I didn't get to be very close to very many of them. Our initial efforts to rent an apartment, my concern with my work, and Silvia's concern about Heather, along with the business of getting adjusted to our apartment, kept us occupied during our first six months in Miami. Another little activity was fencing lessons which we saw

99

advertised in the paper and decided to take because we needed additional exercise and because we had never tried fencing. We enjoyed going to several lessons, but then decided that learning the art was too much like working. Long-term effects came, however, from tennis lessons which Silvia started taking at about this same time. She remembered the days in Cincinnati when she was learning the game and was at my mercy. I thought the lessons were unimportant until she played me a month later and almost beat me.

Both of us were curious about the attitudes that Miami residents had about racial and other current affairs, since the city and its people were unknown to us. Other than the problem of getting into the second apartment, our initial experiences in Miami involving race were virtually nonexistent. Our information came from newspapers, conversations with second or third parties to various problems, and our own observations. Because we were not involved personally in the matters at hand, our discussions were not emotional, and they made our relationship to each other a little bit closer. Silvia acted more as if she were being informed than insulted when I told her about the elementary-level conversation of the gum-snapping Negro women who sat behind me on the bus I took to work. I told Silvia that if these women were any indication, we should recognize that the typical black in Florida could not be thought of in the same terms as the typical black in the northern part of the country where we had always lived.

I also told Silvia about riding on a near-empty bus on which a teenage girl told a friend about riding on a bus one night on which "the only other person was two black fellows. . . They were very good though and didn't do anything to me."

Silvia and I often shared with each other those things about blacks which I heard but a black would not hear, and those things about whites which she heard but which a white would not hear. Miami added a dimension to our listening system, the dimension of language.

Trying to imagine groups with whom we could identify in Miami, we thought almost immediately about the Cuban community, since we had heard over national media they had been discriminated against. We soon found that Miami Cubans were at the opposite end of the socio-economic-educational scale than where most New York Puerto Ricans and blacks are, and the Cubans' attitudes reflected this difference. Silvia got an early introduction to the outlook many Cubans had toward blacks. In response to an advertisement for an apartment during our first month in Miami, Silvia called the designated number, was told the apartment was available, and went immediately to the landlord who turned out to be a Cuban. Upon seeing her, he told her he was not sure the apartment was still available. He said he would have to check with his partner. She said she would be happy to wait. An hour later, another member of the business came. Assuming that a black, obviously an American-born black because she had no Spanish accent, would have no knowledge of any language except English, if she knew that, the other man spoke in Spanish to the landlord. He asked what "that woman was waiting there for." The landlord replied: "Don't worry about her. She came here to rent the apartment we advertised. I told her my partner would be in later today to tell me whether it was still available. Just leave her alone. She'll get tired waiting and leave."

"That made me really mad," Silvia told me that night. "I made up my mind I was going to wait these guys out. So I stayed there all afternoon, asking the landlord every once in a while when the partner was coming in. I didn't get to rent the apartment, but it made me feel good to let them know they could not just push me aside."

We felt close as she told about this incident, just as we always did when running up against discrimination. The nuance I missed, and probably she did too, was that here, as it had been in Fort Greene, it was fine for her to be angered at her group, black or Spanish, but it would be different if I expressed anger at them.

Our getting adjusted in Miami included trips to a variety of churches, including Unitarian, Baptist, Catholic, Methodist and Presbyterian — almost always at least one a week and sometimes two. Soon we began going regularly to Southwest United Presbyterian Church, partly because it was close, partly because

101

Heather liked its excellent Sunday school, and partly because we admired many of the members of the congregation. Rather than the upper-middle class typical of Presbyterian Churches, this small group included primarily manual laborers, tradesmen, and retirees. No one was black and no one spoke Spanish. We both tended to stereotype the members as conservative and perhaps a little bit bigoted. The more we got to know them, however, the more we realized that they were conservative, and the more we realized that they were *not* bigoted. (Reportedly one or two members did leave the church because of our attending, but that rumor was not substantiated.) Silvia, for example, told me about an active member adamantly opposed to busing children in order to integrate schools. This gave Silvia an opportunity to verify my comments to her that many people supporting integration of our society oppose such things as school busing.

By the time we had moved to Miami, I already had decided to remain a Protestant. When we decided to join Southwest Presbyterian Church on November 22, 1970, it was significant not only because it meant a change in church for Silvia, but also because it was the first time either of us had joined a church since marriage. This fact made us close, and like so many things that made us close, it made us a little bit closer than it otherwise would because we were of different colors. Besides that, we both had a sense of accomplishment in her being the one black in that church, at least at that time.

The all-too-frequent event happened in the spring of 1970 — I was fired because my copy editing had not been up to the standards of the *News* during my six-month trial period. The news should have been devastating in view of my having recently resigned from a good-paying job in New York — to spend $500 moving to Miami to accept a lower-paying job, and then to lose it in six months. Naturally I was not delighted, but it did convince me not to try to be a copy editor just because I wanted to be a newspaperman. I immediately started writing job application letters, but because I had a bad employment record and had just been fired, because I was convinced I could not edit copy, and because I did not have the driver's license

102

necessary for most reporting jobs, my possibilities were seriously limited. I had already made an attempt to obtain a Florida driver's license and been told to wait two years. We lived for a couple of weeks on our federal income tax refund, a week on our New York state tax refund, and then I started drawing unemployment compensation.

We heard that the Catholic Church needed a couple to help supervise a home on Miami Beach it operated for girls who had recently stopped using narcotics. Since my letters of application for various newspaper jobs had been rejected, I thought this center would be a good place for Silvia and me to make use of our previous experience with narcotics addicts, since the job did not require professional training. We talked to the two nuns who supervised the home and to the doctor who directed it, and we were told we would probably start work the next week. For once we got things ready early, boxing up most of our belongings and stacking them in the living room in preparation for our move to Miami Beach. But we didn't move, because we were told a couple days later that the other couple under consideration had been selected.

The good offshoot of this business was that one of the nuns, aware of my newspaper background, had arranged for me to work for *The Voice*, a tabloid weekly published by the Archdiocese of Miami and having a circulation of 80,000. The editor said he would pay me $35 a story for about four stories a week. The pay was nothing to get excited about, but the type of job did excite me. I was told to write about issues not directly involving the church but having religious or moral or social significance. I wrote about a ghetto day-care center that needed support, interviewed teenagers as to why they start on dope, and did stories on a wide variety of other issues. About a third of my stories weren't used. One involved a black victim of police prejudice during the June, 1970 race riots in Miami, and was documented with court testimony and quotes from a priest. I later sold the story to the *Associated Press*, but they did not use it.

My best story, an investigation into the cause of those riots, seemed easy to me because I had lived with a black long enough

103

to feel free to talk with blacks, including two teenagers who threatened me with lead pipes. Silvia and I enjoyed talking about my *Voice* stories, particularly those with racial significance. I probably made the same mistake regarding this enjoyment that I had made with *The Fort Greene Observer*, however, and that was assuming that I was benefiting her personally by writing stories favorable to her race.

Regardless of the social import of the stories, $35 a piece wasn't much to live on, so Silvia took a part-time job working for a summer church school program. One of my stories *The Voice* had a particularly good reason not to publish was about an encounter group Silvia and I attended for half price, with the understanding that I would write about it. The encounter, conducted by a local psychologist, involved blunt discussion among the fourteen participants, included among whom were two other psychologists. Silvia and I, who had attended a sixty-minute encounter conducted by the same psychologist at the Unitarian Church, looked forward to this twenty-four hour job because we were curious about it. We both mentioned that our biracial nature might have encouraged our going to this otherwise all-white event, but that was certainly not a major reason for our going. The psychologists, however, kept asking us, particularly me, about our biracial marriage.

"I think you are ashamed at being married to a black," one of the psychologists told me soon after the thing began. I responded to this as I had to all the charges at the encounter dealing with biracial marriage — quickly, articulately, and confidently, not sure whether the psychologist was dumb enough to ignore the irrationality of what he said, bigoted enough to ignore the irrationality of what he said, or playing a game with me to see what reaction other participants had to such ridiculous thoughts.

In the early hours of that Sunday morning, as we continued to sit on the floor of the psychologist's home talking about ourselves, various group members were induced to stand up and move around the room pretending to do something they would be doing somewhere else and doing it in the way they liked. When Silvia's turn came, she danced around the room madly.

104

"I figured that was what she'd do," I said as soon as she stopped. "She's always telling me how she likes to dance and how much she danced when she was a girl."

A psychologist surprised me by saying quickly that I had insulted Silvia's culture. I replied that I was merely stating a fact, the fact that she always had liked to dance. "That doesn't mean I'm insulting her or her culture! "

Within a year I'd find out the psychologist was right about this. I did regard dancing, at least a great enthusiasm for it, as a reflection of Spanish and black emotionalism, which I did not understand or respect. Before we were married, I went to a couple of Spanish dances with Silvia to be "openminded and adventuresome." She didn't complain about not going to more, because we enjoyed each other no matter what we did. Once we got married, I ignored my previous implication that I'd learn how to dance. Besides that, I saw no need for dancing after marriage, since we could then do horizontally what is done vertically on the dance floor. In Ohio and Pennsylvania we had been a long way from any Spanish music, in Fort Greene we had not had time for it. Now there was time and plenty of Spanish music and Silvia's blood was getting hot for the music and the dance floor. A cultural difference that had been submerged was coming to light.

When Silvia and I were home the following evening and discussing the encounter after we had gone to bed, we both expressed curiosity about the emphasis put on our biracialness. I asked her if she felt I had problems with biracialness as they had charged. She said no. I felt close to Silvia when she then told me: "I was proud of you the way you stood up to all of those accusations about interracial marriage and answered their charges like you did. It took a strong-willed person to do that. It made me feel good."

One of the messages that would have been most helpful to me was something the psychologist had told me after the session had ended. She told me to "quit being so negative. Silvia has such a great potential if you'd stop being so negative."

I rejected the advise about negativeness because I had no idea how negative my thinking had become. The negativeness had been increasing gradually since my high school days and had gone un-noticed. Being married to a black, even a very positive one, had increased my negativeness because I thought the black had to say "Yes Master," and her white spouse therefore was obliged to say "No" with extra fervor. I rejected the psychologist's strong emphasis on Silvia's potential as a meaningless gesture precipitated only by a sense of propriety in saying something nice about a black. This attitude that any compliment to Silvia was a mere gesture to be nice to the black became increasingly predominant in my thinking in subsequent years.

My working for *The Voice* also enabled us to attend another encounter, one that had no similarities to the other. This was a marriage encounter sponsored by the Catholic Church, which we were invited to attend because I wanted to write a story about it. We enjoyed the weekend very much because of the Christian spirit of the couples there (all of them white), because of the good lay and clerical leadership, and particularly because it told us again that we had a very successful marriage. In answer to the question of why she wanted to go on living with me, Silvia wrote: "For the same reasons I married you. Your genuineness, sincerity, your lack of fear. The warm and true way in which sometimes I feel your love, (I failed to catch the significance of the "sometimes.") I feel you have helped me grow as a person and will continue to do so."

In answer to the same question, I wrote: "I have a great deal in common with you and have many common goals with you. I feel we know each other well and so can be of considerable help to each other. I think we have rapidly increased our knowledge of each other in seven years. . ."

The leaders told us that at times during the two-day encounter, spouses would get very angry at each other. Silvia was infuriated at my answer to the question of what most separated us. I wrote: "Your increasing tendency in the last year or two to regard me as the typical middle class white who fails to give you middle class conveniences, not because we cannot afford them but because I lack consideration for you. . . . Fact of the matter is that even if we could afford them, I wouldn't want you to have them because I didn't marry you on that basis. . ."

She told me hotly that she did not want luxuries, but did not see why she could not have some of the conveniences enjoyed by other women. She became angrier when I told her she was better off economically than she had ever been.

My lack of diplomacy in making that remark is beside the point. The problem was that I thought someone who had once lived in a slum should be content with anything that was somewhat better — even though not a lot better; and that was not the case. Many husbands tell their wives that they expect too much in the way of household goods; but that's just a financial argument, even though perhaps a hot one. It gets more complicated when a husband tells his once-poor wife that she should be content with what she has because it's more than her mother had. Emotion is added when the husband is white and the once-poor wife is black. Although this factor started to emerge in Fort Greene, this encounter was the first place we really began to realize the very different outlook I had on Silvia's premarital financial condition, as opposed to the outlook she had on it. The encounter for the most part, however, documented the strong love between us, or seeming to exist between us.

Realizing the need for income, I did such things as sell a feature story to *The Miami Herald*, and do a week's worth of public relations work for the Catholic War Veterans at their Miami Beach convention. But I failed to find any full-time job in Miami where I could use my journalistic talents.

"I'm going to see what I can get for a job," Silvia told me in August. "I've already contacted a couple of places."

I wasn't against the idea, but my concern was getting a job for myself so I could support the family. If she got a job, it could serve as a subsidiary income. Actually she did get one, and got it quickly. The University of Miami needed an interviewer in its personnel department, and preferred someone who could speak Spanish in view of Miami's fast-growing Spanish population, or someone who was black to meet federal requirements for increased employment of minorities. Silvia filled the bill all around with her experience in employment counseling, fluency in Spanish, and her black complexion.

I was as delighted as she about the job. It only paid $7,000, but that was better than nothing. Just as important, since she would be helping people get jobs, particularly minorities, her job would serve a human need. Besides that, we recognized it as an opportunity from which to build her career.

Her working and my unemployment meant that I was home, partly as a maid and partly as a writer of job application letters. I didn't mind a little maid's work for a little while, since this was the best way to serve the three of us at the moment. Soon I began to hate it and did almost no maid work, but Silvia understood and had time to clean up our three-and-one-half-room apartment.

Silvia and I visited nightly about her new job, finding the conversation mutually interesting, particularly so since much of it involved the employment of minorities, or the lack thereof. At first I shared her suspicion and anger about alleged discrimination. Within several months, however, I began to think she was getting overly suspicious, and told her so. She resented this.

Since my only contact with the Miami professional world had been with a newspaper — a very liberal one at that — I had seen no evidence of job discrimination. And, ironically, it was my knowledge that I would not engage in such discrimination that made me challenge my wife's contention that others engaged in it.

During the last week of February, 1971, my job application letters and interviews resulted in my being hired by Mount Sinai Hospital on Miami Beach to publish an employee newspaper. The salary was not lucrative, only about $7,000 a year, but coupled with Silvia's salary would give us more than enough on which to live. More important, it would get me out of the house and busy working. After being told Friday I had been hired — I think it was February 28 — I was told to report Monday morning. "Every new employee here has to have a physical before starting work. We've scheduled yours for tomorrow morning. Is that O.K.?" my boss-to-be told me.

I said yes and that I looked forward to seeing her Monday. Saturday morning when I told the doctor examining me that I had had a convulsion the night before, she jumped back and expressed alarm in her broken English. She told me that I had

108

failed for that reason.

When I called the hospital Monday to try to rescue my job, I was not allowed to talk to my boss-to-be, whom I had clearly told about my diabetic condition during the employment interview the previous week. I then told the hospital to whom I was speaking that maybe the Cuban doctor examining me had misunderstood something I had said about my diabetes or my convulsion. They told me she was licensed in the United States, had failed me for the physical, and the hospital regarded the doctor's word as final.

This infuriated me. It depressed me. My dad had warned me about employment problems I might have because of my diabetes, but I thought he was being overly worrisome. "Maybe he was right," I told my mother who happened to be visiting us. My diabetes had handicapped my employment for six years now, but this was primarily because of the driving problem. Lately several newspapers had rejected me because of a policy of not hiring diabetics because of a possible effect on group insurance rates. Even if they didn't have better sense, so be it. But when a medical institution, a place where people go to make their bodies functional in spite of disease, refuses to hire those who have already been treated and are capable of functioning like any other employee, it mixed me up.

"If that's the attitude they have, they should tell people at Mt. Sinai they might as well go ahead and die, because once their ailment is controlled, they won't be able to do anything anyway," I said bitterly to Silvia. She agreed. Having just experienced a certain sort of discrimination, it was easy to discuss the event with a wife who had experienced discrimination of a different sort.

In telling me the news of people with whom she worked, Silvia frequently told me about one person getting a federal grant and another person not getting one. I got tired of it. She started suggesting I should apply for a federal grant, since everybody seemed to be getting them. "Go ahead and write a proposal," she told me.

The term "proposal" was foreign to me. I was too idealistic and too stupid to realize that all sorts of government money could be gotten by people with no more credentials than I had. I resented these frequent suggestions, feeling that she was misinformed to think the government handed out money to anybody who had what they made sound like a worthwhile project. If it had ended here, my ignorance would have cost nothing except a potential source of income. However, ignorance plus a black spouse created marital friction. I told her grants like that were not earned by anybody but were just bribes the government gave to a few blacks to help shut up the great majority of blacks. Naturally Silvia did not like those charges, even though there was enough truth in them that she would have accepted them from a black spouse.

Unable to be the family's breadwinner, I decided to assume the traditional "mother's job" of teaching Bible school during June, 1971. My doing an excellent job of teaching and directing my teenagers' portion of the closing program gave me a good feeling, particularly when my wife praised me. Since we didn't have much else to celebrate, and since we had seen almost none of Florida, we decided to spend that weekend visiting Cape Kennedy and the center of the state. Saturday night when traveling on a back road in central Florida, the shortage of eating places forced us to drive up to a second class seafood house. Silvia had just turned off the ignition when the apparent owner of the place jumped up from her outdoor seat and ran toward us. As we got out of the car, she scowled at us: "No. No. We're not open."

When she had run to within three car lengths of us and I had gotten out of our car and started walking toward the restaurant, she told me: "I'll serve them, but you'll have to stay in the car. I don't approve of this."

Apparently she thought refusing to serve me would not make her guilty of racial discrimination, but would at the same time make things inconvenient for us, and would also allow her to convince me and her friends sitting nearby that she was opposed to my being married to a black. In any event, it was time for me to eat and I was content to let her rest in her stupidity while we found another place. Silvia was less practical and more ideological. In that sense it was like our battle to get a Fort Greene

110

apartment, rather than the Louisville affair, where I was the more ideological, and she the more practical. Perhaps in Fort Greene and here, it was the matter of the discrimination having been directly against her rather than against some other black. Silvia lectured the woman:

"I don't think it's very Christian of you to do this. And it's not very American either — particularly when it's the Fourth of July."

Silvia called the police, while I waited patiently in the car with Heather, but they referred her to the county sheriff, who said there was nothing he could do since the restaurant was a private business. I assured Silvia that he was wrong, but she agreed with me there was no way we were going to overturn the sentiments of the local authorities, at least that evening. The next place we found was an interesting pancake house. The food was excellent, but not quite as good as the time we had telling the owner about our incident at the other restaurant.

Although blatant racism, such as this "Independence Day Incident," consisted mainly in isolated events, particularly within the confines of Miami, we were coming to realize that just because we were not conscious of being different colors did not mean that others were not. This message came not from those hostile to biracial marriages, for they, like New Yorkers and other urbanites, did not express their racism to us. The message came, rather, from our friends. It came from friends in our church who, although not bothered by our biracialness, felt it necessary to express to us that they were not bothered by it. The indication that our society did notice us as different came from the school teacher friend who automatically started talking about biracial marriage almost every time he saw us. The message came perhaps most convincingly from the eight-year-old son of a very liberal and friendly couple in whose home we were visiting, when after supper he came to me and asked:

"Is that your wife?"

When I told him it was, he interjected: "But she's black."

Since we could live comfortably on Silvia's salary plus my occasional earnings, I suggested to Silvia the possibility of inviting her sister, Hilda, to visit us again, particularly since

111

Hilda was becoming more interested in her boy friend than in her schoolwork. Once I supplied the initiative, Silvia carried out the idea. Unfortunately, Hilda's four-month visit turned out to be little more profitable than her visit to us in Ohio. In both cases I had exhibited a sense of responsibility and moral obligation. But my good intentions were not enough. In Florida, as in Ohio, once Hilda arrived I tried to help out by treating her as I thought teenagers should be treated. Most of the differences between us were due to the generation gap, but I attributed many of them to our cultural differences. An example was her buying a transistor radio with money she earned as a waitress at Kentucky Fried Chicken. Ignoring the popularity of such radios among today's youth, I told Silvia it showed her sister's excessive craving for music, apparently a product of her Spanish or black culture. Silvia didn't say anything, but she told me later she did not agree. Our biracial marriage had converted a mere problem of generation gap into a cultural issue.

In mid-1971, still without a job, I agreed with Silvia that it would be good for all four of us if I could work in my mother's clothing store for a few months. Mother said she could use the extra help, so I flew to Clarksville, intending to help her build up her sales volume in anticipation of sale of the store, and I planned to do some job hunting at the same time. While I was there, the Illinois Chamber of Commerce asked me to go to Chicago for an interview, but afterwards decided (quite wisely) that the philosophy of the Chamber of Commerce was not reflected in my thinking, in spite of my efforts to make it seem so.

I also thought seriously about trying to buy a rural weekly newspaper near where my mother lived, even though Silvia had said she would never move there. I figured that if I made such a purchase and got the paper going successfully, she'd change her mind. I thought she was being somewhat narrow minded, even a little bigoted, in saying she didn't want to live in a small town. Of course I'd told her before we got married that I did not intend to live in a small town and could understand why she might not like to do so, but things had changed since then.

One Friday night that fall, I don't remember when, I thought

112

about my life as I sat in a Clarksville cafe eating supper before returning to work in the store that evening. In a way I seemed so different from what I had been when during my high school days I had sat in the same restaurant waiting to go back to work in the same store. I now had a wife and daughter. I now had no father. I had extended much energy during those intervening thirteen or fourteen years, and had apparently gained little from it. Yet in a way I was not so different. Even though I had lost jobs and stood in unemployment lines, I still knew how to work hard, just as I had when I was in high school. I had been cold to many people in New York and Florida, yet I still had the same friendliness that enabled me to greet almost everybody that came into the restaurant. I read with vigor the national as well as the state news in the *Des Moines Register* next to my plate, even though during the last year I had made an effort to ignore daily newspapers because I felt my knowledge of world events to be unimportant. As I left a small tip for the waitress-cashier and exchanged a few genuinely friendly comments with her, I knew I had not lost my warmth toward small town waitresses, even though waitresses in cities had become but machines to me. As I smiled — I had found out during my several months in Clarksville that I did still like to smile — and walked out the door into a brisk wind, I realized again I had the same vigor I had always prided myself in having, but seemed to have lost in Miami, if not on the streets of New York.

I then remembered a pleasant visit I had had several Sunday afternoons earlier with a close friend who had graduated with me from high school. A mathematics professor at a nearby college, this friend mentioned during his conversation that initially he had withdrawn from college after one term — "the small-town boy having problems adjusting to the city," he explained. I had always heard about the problems of anyone moving from one environment to another, but had never taken them too seriously. Maybe I was finding out at thirty-one what he had come to recognize at eighteen — that it is not easy to move from one culture to another, no matter who you are. Maybe my problems in changing cultures were not that I was less a man than I had once thought: maybe the challenge of change was greater than I had once thought.

I walked on across the street and back to the job of selling clothing. On other evenings I worked in the woodworking shop I had built up since childhood. I made Heather a desk and stove out of wood I had gotten free during my high school days. Arriving in Clarksville for Christmas, Silvia was as delighted as Heather when they saw these gifts.

I had always been taught to buy things locally from good dealers, so I had purchased, largely with my mother's money, a new Plymouth to transport us back to Miami. Silvia and I agreed that I should forget about newspapering in view of the problem with driver's licenses, and should go back to school. Since mathematics had always been my strongest subject, even though I had only one calculus course in college, I decided the best way to make use of my mathematical ability was to go into accounting.

I started attending the University of Miami in January, trying to make up for lost time by taking eighteen hours, all of it accounting courses or courses needed to qualify for the C.P.A. examination. It seemed good to be going to school again, and I was thankful my wife's working at the university enabled me to attend there at greatly reduced cost. It became frustrating, however, as the B+ student of 1960 seemed to be the C student of 1972, even though I studied hard for my courses in Miami.

Silvia told me in February she was being very seriously considered for the position of assistant director of the University of Miami's Affirmative Action Programs, a program the federal government requires major recipients of its aid to operate in order to continue receiving the aid. The program is designed to assure that minority groups and women are hired in adequate numbers and given an equal opportunity to obtain responsible positions.

Silvia left me in the car while making the final arrangements with the director of the program and Dr. Henry King Stanford, president of the university. When she came back she smiled quietly and told me that she had been hired for $12,000 a year, both of us were joyous. That was more money than either of us had ever made, and so even Silvia's tight husband said we should go out and eat a meal to celebrate. I was as happy as Silvia, not merely because of the money, but because this seemed like a great opportunity to eliminate injustices and prevent future ones.

We had been discussing for a year the possibility of buying a house. Her new job and my enrollment in school made it clear that we were going to be in Miami for some time, so in May our shopping came to an end when we purchased a $29,000 home within twenty minutes distance of the university. This purchase was a first-time experience for us, and a very pleasant one. It was an interesting contrast to our difficulty at renting a home. We found that in buying a home, black skin was not nearly as important as green dollars; and we had those thanks to a loan from my mother.

We both felt a sense of accomplishment in bringing the first black onto a previously all-white street, and then showing that we mowed our lawn and put out our trash like anybody else. Perhaps I, more than Silvia, was conscious of the fact that this accomplishment was possible, or at least easier, because of my family's money. Anyway, we were now happily settled — and pleasantly amused by the neighbor who apologetically explained to us that she had been planning to put up a fence between our property and hers for some six or seven years, but just hadn't had time to get it done until the week after we moved in.

CHAPTER VII

The Woman Wears The Pants

"You embarrassed me today. You had no business saying anything," Silvia scolded me minutes after she got home from work. She was too business-like to yell at me, too mad not to speak in a loud growl. She was too distant for me to imagine, too close to avoid, too aloof to talk down to, too much on the same level to talk up to. Her words were cold, they were hot, they boiled as she turned on the stove.

"You should *not* have questioned what my boss said — particularly when you didn't know anything about what you were talking about." She was not suggesting I had been ignorant, she was telling me so.

Surprised, somewhat insulted, disbelieving, I responded: "Well why do you say that? Ted [that's her boss] knows me. I think he respects me a little bit. He isn't going to mind if I disagree with him. I thought he'd appreciate my viewpoint."

"You're saying that you have talked with him in an informal setting. That's different. He had come into my office to tell me something and it was not appropriate for you, just because you happened to be there, to start questioning what he said."

It was October or November of 1972. I had not yet learned that if Silvia had not always been independent, she was now, that if she always wanted my advice as I once thought she did, that was no longer the case.

The conversation involved an unimportant incident in her office that day when I happened to be there between classes. When her boss came in and told her something, I questioned him. I thought I was adding a third dimension to his directions

116

by telling about comments white professors had made to me that they could not have made to a black. That it was not my place to speak, despite my good intensions, could well have been the case.

However, it seemed that Silvia's message to me was clear: "Let me run my office myself." Until then I had considered my brain and perspective at least a small part of the reason for the success of Silvia Huber in her job of dealing with frictions among races. I thought she *wanted* my opinions and ideas, not that she just tolerated them. I thought that when I had typed a couple reports she needed for her job, she had appreciated my additions and revisions. Now I wondered if she had thanked me just because I was her secretary rather than her literary and historical consultant.

Silvia had established herself as the professional person in the family, and I was the follower. Our roles had been reversed from what I had always expected them to be, and the pain was complicated by several factors. My self image had decreased rather than increased since starting school in January, 1972, as I got mostly C's in my schoolwork rather than the A's I had expected. Part of the reason was that in the Spring semester I had tried to "make up for lost time" by taking eighteen hours of courses that are prerequisites for the exam for Certified Public Accountants, and half of these were out of sequence. But this excuse was getting old by the summer session. As my initial delight at returning to school declined and frustration increased, Silvia became less the spouse whose job made it possible for me to attend school and more the parent having to support a stumbling youngster.

At the same time that my self image declined, Silvia's increased. She had some administrative responsibility for the first time in her life. She worked at times with some of the more powerful people at the university, including its president. She guarded her self image as most any new executive, but I think she guarded it much more adamantly because she was black and because she was a woman, as suggested by the many hours with me she spent comparing her performance to that of whites and men. This created friction between us, because I would frequently argue that white males couldn't be wrong all the time.

I couldn't help but be happy when Silvia showed me page 35 of the June 3, 1972 *New York Times*. The three-column picture of her talking to two women at The Americana Hotel the day before — at a conference on equal opportunity for women in business — made me proud of what she was doing. Yet it made me a little jealous, since I would like to have had some recognition for doing something or other. It didn't seem as if there was so much difference between our abilities or the energy we had exerted. Maybe the only significant difference was that she was black, and so she needed lesser qualifications than I to get into a position where she was recognized. She told me when showing the picture that she suspected part of the reason she was in the photo was that she was black. But she strongly resented my suggestions that she appeared there because she was black and Spanish. These suggestions became increasingly frequent as I tried to find an explanation as to why my wife was more successful than I.

Several months later Silvia was participating on a panel at a similar conference. There again, as with her being interviewed five minutes on a Miami TV station, I was proud but jealous. Such jealousy appears in many marriages. Here, however, the problem was more difficult because I realized that her blackness was part of the reason she was recognized. When I went to the extreme of attributing most of her success to her color and her Spanish heritage, she went to the opposite extreme of saying it had nothing to do with it. Bitterness resulted. The increase in our differences during 1973 about the relationship among color, gender, and success of Silvia and other blacks and women was stimulated by several conferences she attended. Whereas the first several of them to which she went were delights to both of us, I now felt that the conference participants were so adamant as to make her suspicious of all whites and all males.

In a letter in 1972, Mrs. Vitti, our Fort Greene landlady, wished us well and told us the current situation in their family — a glum situation because of the increased lawbreaking in the area. Although she didn't put it in these words, obviously they felt increasingly alienated from the area as there was a continuing decline in the population of whites, and as the hostility toward them increased. She told about the radiator stolen from their car and about something else being stolen from it shortly after that, and she wrote also about the burden of Mr. Vitti's continuing to have to have two jobs in order to support two daughters and send them to a parochial school because of fear of what would happen to them in the public schools, physically and academically.

Silvia had previously defended with the same argument about the public schools the fact Benedicta sent her children to parochial schools. When expressing my concern about the Vitti family to Silvia, I thought she was indifferent. Two times when she visited Benedicta after that, while attending conferences in New York, I suggested she visit the Vittis. She never did. This angered me. I knew she could have conveniently visited them since their house was only about ten blocks from Benedicta's apartment. That's why I didn't go for her excuse that she had not had time to go over there, particularly after visiting with her relatives — Spanish style (that's talking until the sun starts to rise). If Silvia wasn't going to visit them, she could at least have the guts to give me a straight explanation; and that apparently would have been that she was not going to be friendly to them because they had discriminated against her. And it was Silvia who was always telling me to let bygones be bygones.

My sense of warmth for the Vittis and my contempt for Silvia's not visiting them — I hadn't been back to New York since we had left in 1969 — was stimulated everytime we cleaned Heather's bedroom, because Silvia always wanted to throw out the two dolls the Vitti girls had given Heather in 1969. Once I questioned Silvia: "Do you want to throw them away because they remind you of the Vittis, or because the dolls are white."

"Heather doesn't play with them any more."

"How come if she doesn't play with dolls anymore, you bought her that black one?" I asked as the tension built.

"That's the kind of doll girls her age play with," Silvia replied. "Those real big ones the Vittis gave her are the kind girls use when they're older."

119

I didn't believe her. She had spent too much time fussing about Heather having white dolls and not black dolls. Whether she was telling the truth is beside the point. The problem was that the insignificant matter of which dolls daughter really likes had resulted in an emotional argument.

In early 1971 we were given free tickets to the annual $100-a-plate dinner of the Miami Chapter of the National Conference of Christians and Jews. We had fun. It certainly was a new experience seeing rich people gathered together in a huge dining room of an elegant Miami Beach Hotel. We agreed that the conference director had invited us not only because he was our personal friend, but also because Silvia's black face was appropriate for the occasion. This was another instance in which we were having a good time enjoying the fruits of our combined resources — in this case Silvia's black skin. At the 1972 dinner our attitude was about the same. Arthur Godfrey's speech was not very informative, but it was still an evening out amidst pleasant surroundings and an opportunity to visit with many interesting people, most of whose political views were quite similar to ours and whose incomes were quite different from ours.

By the 1973 dinner there was a little different relationship between us. We had a much better table. I had finished my accounting courses but still had no regular job. We had a good time, but as the other five or six men at our table told about their jobs and since I did not have much of a one to talk about — and couldn't even say that I was a student — I had a sense of inferiority to Silvia as well as to them. This wasn't helped any when, after Senator John Tunney gave a good speech, Silvia and I went up to the podium to try to shake his hand.

Tunney made a special effort to greet her; but even though I was standing right beside her, I had to chase him to give him a quick handshake and compliment. Silvia and I agreed afterward it was her blackness that made the difference. Tunney's actions, which were a matter of necessity, not choice, were to say nice things to the Jews and white gentile guests from the area's upper crust, and then to be friendly to any minority persons present. But I was frustrated by Silvia's having a place, even though small, in the overall picture, while I seemed to have no place — not even that of the newspaperman asking Tunney a couple of questions. I had this same feeling at that dinner when Silvia, getting increasingly nervy these days, went up to Maurice Ferre, the multi-millionaire Puerto Rican who was to become mayor of Miami within a year, and spoke to him. The fact they started their conversation in Spanish was not a factor; I felt just as much out of it when they switched to English a few words later.

Where I really could have used a knowledge of Spanish was in the job market, because by 1972 the Cuban minority was becoming a majority and businesses wanted bilingual people. After unsuccessful efforts during the summer to get a part-time accounting job while finishing at the university, I got a part-time job in the fall with a small C.P.A. firm. This restored my confidence somewhat, but it made me feel no less subservient to Silvia because she had put me in touch with the C.P.A., had gone with me on the job interview, and frequently had to transport me to and from work. I got a part-time job in early 1973 doing individual income tax returns, but here again I was dependent on her much of the time for transportation.

About this time I applied for an accounting job with a public health agency serving low income persons in the black ghetto of northwest Miami. This seemed to be an ideal situation — a good place to use my experience in associating with blacks, poor blacks included, a good place to satisfy my idealistic desires to help the less fortunate, and a job for which I was more qualified than would be most any other accountant, black or white, willing to work for $7,000 a year. The chief accountant, who was white, liked me and indicated he wanted to hire me as soon as he could get the O.K. from Mr. M_____, the director. Mr. M_____, who was black, was busy that day and so I would have to come back. On the return visit, Mr. M_____ managed to find thirty seconds to raise his arm, clothed in an expensive-looking knit suit coat, and shake hands. The meeting over, I left. A few days later I went back and the chief accountant, shaking his head, said he was sorry I didn't get the job because he felt I would have done it well, but he explained

121

he did not have the final say.

There was no problem at home that night. It was reassuring to have my black wife agree with me that apparently I had been discriminated against. In coming months, however, I would remember that incident and refer to it too frequently in responding to her condemnation of white employers discriminating against blacks.

In July, 1973, I was employed as an accountant by Aristar, Inc. — at that time called the Family Finance Corporation — a nation-wide conglomerate concentrating in the small-loan business. It made everyone in the family happy, Heather included, to have me working on a full-time basis for the first time since 1970. This was my first venture into the corporate world, and we enjoyed visiting about it a number of evenings. It was also my first opportunity to hear women bookkeepers and secretaries of all ages refered to as "girls". I saw indications of racial prejudice. A year earlier I had told Silvia she was getting carried away in believing discrimination against minorities and women existed on a significant basis throughout Miami; but I admitted to her that now that I had gotten out into the real world, her views were much closer to the truth than I had realized them to be. For two or three months, she enjoyed listening to my stories of racism as I suspected it to exist at my employer's.

Silvia had told me as soon as I was hired not to make known the color of my wife; and it soon became apparent that that was good advice. I remember an additional bookkeeping machine operator, a black in her twenties, hired during a particularly busy time. Perhaps because of the time pressure being put on the two normally very kind and amiable machine operators with whom she was working, perhaps because of some shortcoming in the black woman's personality or technical abilities, friction developed and she was fired. As the head of the bookkeeping department discussed the matter with me and the two machine operators whom he had known for years, he said: "I'm not prejudiced against blacks, but. . . "

I discretely refrained from saying anything out of place in that conversation, but I often found that when my superiors

122

showed contempt for blacks — contempt so overt they could not have indicated it if I had been black rather than half of a black-white marriage — it was sometimes hard to go back to thinking about accounting and respecting the knowledge and authority of my superiors as I would otherwise have done. It was a feeling something like that which I'd had while being interviewed six years earlier for a job on a middlewest newspaper. I had been impressed with the editor as well as the paper until he made a comment about Puerto Ricans that could have been interpreted as hostile. After that, it was difficult for me to appreciate fully the man's qualities. The publisher's assistant asked my wife's ethnic background a few minutes later, and when I said she was Puerto Rican, I seemed to connect that with the editor's remark, even though I said nothing in words.

Some of the events at Aristar that had racial overtones were much less serious. At lunch one day an employee who moved with the company when it was relocated from Delaware to Miami a decade earlier, was going through his frequent post-lunch discourse on the wide number and variety of prostitutes he had hired. He accentuated this by describing some of them, saying he had had sexual relations — that's not the word he used — with almost every*thing*, even a nigger.

The employee sitting opposite me, unbothered by the idea of prostitution, shook his head and said very piously: "That's something I'd never do." He shook his head again and asked me: "Pat — would you ever screw a nigger?"

Realizing this was no time to discuss the psychology or philosophy of interracial marriage or interracial intercourse, I shrugged my shoulders.

Naturally I did not agree with fellow employees when they demeaned blacks, and I worked hard to gently challenge such attitudes, both on the job and at the lunch table. I worked almost as hard to regard women as equals — sometimes risking being considered unusual by calling a female employee a woman rather than a girl. After doing this during the day, I'd often go home to hear Silvia tell me I didn't respect women or blacks. This charge would have been easier to accept if I had been anti-black or anti-female during the day. Believing, rightly or wrongly, that I had stuck out my neck for both blacks and women during the day made it particularly frustrating to be called a white male chauvanist at home.

The feeling of the right thing being said to the wrong person was the same I had had in November, 1972, when upon going to Silvia's office at the end of a work day, she asked if we could lend some money to a poor woman whose landlord was about to evict her and her two children. When I said I thought we should help but then went ahead to question the woman as to what her plans were for the future, Silvia angrily took me aside and scolded me:

"The woman needs money. Why are you questioning? You are humiliating her by asking her all those questions!"

Of course the woman was black. I think Silvia pictured me as the brutal white having no respect for this woman because she was black. Anyway, after a little more conversation I proposed we lend the woman $212 — her back rent plus 1 month, rather than the $350 Silvia proposed. After she got the woman a job within a few days and the woman quit it within a week, and after Silvia had found out a little more about the woman, my wife told me she was glad I had limited our loan and wished we had loaned her nothing at all.

A much bigger investment loss also began in November, 1972 — our first investment in common stock. I considered myself the family member with the most knowledge of finance, and the custodian of our resources — even though Silvia was supporting us. Silvia was shocked when I told her I had purchased $4000 worth of stock, but she did not mind my doing it once I assured her it was O.K. I gave her authoritative discourses on the stock market — even though I knew little about it — and I gathered that she appreciated my talk since she knew nothing about the market. She got more relaxed and I more confident as the value of our stock approached $4800. Now that I had taught her how to interpret the stock pages, she noticed in January, 1973, that our stock had gone back to its purchase price and a little bit lower. She became slightly concerned. I, the expert, said this was the time to invest more, so we bought another $20,000 worth of the same stock.

124

The price kept going down. At first it was just an interesting point of conversation. When the shares we had purchased in the $40's went down to around $30 a share, she started wondering but did not express any concern. But as it dropped into the $20's on its way to below $10 a share, she began referring to it in criticism of me. She said I should not be so tight about buying new furniture or spending money on other things she wanted when her proposed expenditures were minimal compared to what we had lost in stock. I came back ethnically, saying if she had an understanding of finance and business and the Protestant work ethic — as most blacks and Puerto Ricans did not — she would realize that a loss in an investment cannot be compared to an expenditure for a personal item.

"When my grandfather sold suits during the depression at less than he paid for them, he didn't tell his wife they might as well spend money on personal items rather than invest in a losing business. He knew that an investment was different than a personal expenditure and so he bought more suits in spite of the risk of losing money on them too."

"If my point was valid, it was obscured by the ethnic implications of my little speech. Worst of all, marital conflict was encouraged. Perhaps this is another example of how difficult it is for the biracial partner to speak favorably of the principles of his culture, and yet not alienate himself from the culture of his spouse — and ultimately from the spouse herself.

In the fall of 1973 we realized that our relationship was not as good as it once was, and we decided to attend another Cathloic marriage encounter. We agreed that our relationship had deteriorated since our first encounter one and one-half years earlier. In fact, when asked to list the events which we had enjoyed doing together, neither of us mentioned anything occuring since we had moved to Miami. Out of a list of twenty-five indications of friction within a marriage, we each listed about fifteen things wrong in ours. This list included frequent quarrels, ridiculing and insulting each other, and indifference to each other's problems.

Silvia wrote that after going along with all the things I had wanted to do since we had been married and "not getting any appreciation for it," she had turned to fulfilling herself, "thinking more of what I want to do and get out of life."

I could understand this except for her saying she had gone along with me in helping publish *The Fort Greene Observer*. When I said this was our project, not mine, she disagreed. She seemed to have forgotten that the *Observer* was for "her" people, in her old neighborhood.

In addition to attacking my concern about money, she condemned a proposal I had made a month earlier that we save all we could while both working for ten years, in order to have capital to start a weekly newspaper. She said that this "makes me feel like you are expecting that we devote all our efforts to engage in a venture to satisfy your lifelong dream. I feel this is good for Pat. I feel left out."

She had told me affectionately only two years earlier that she knew I liked to write and wouldn't mind supporting the family while I wrote. So now her opposition to a newspaper seemed like a double cross. Besides that, it made me think she was more the short-sighted black or Puerto Rican than I thought I married. She didn't seem to have that WASP or Jewish ability to realize that worthwhile ventures take long-range planning and hard work.

Part of the reason I married Silvia was because she had broad ambitions. By 1973 her perspective had gotten much much wider. She wrote at the marriage encounter:

"I feel that there are a lot of things I want to do that I haven't yet done. Like finish my degree or maybe some day if I'm interested enough in some project or subject, go for a PhD. I also want to learn to paint, do ceramics, try some needlework, do a lot of reading — fiction and non-fiction. Eventually I may want to go into some aspect of teaching. I have considered many careers and yet have found no sure one."

At times I thought these very broad ambitions were good. That's why, for example, I spent several nights writing her application for the President's Commission of White House Fellows. At other times I considered her ambitions impractical, even ridiculous. When I so thought, often I accused her of thinking she could be a big success in the world, when in fact

126

her accomplishments were almost entirely limited to a job designed for a minority person dealing with other minority group members and a few whites involved with minorities. It is difficult enough for any man in this decade to belittle the potentialities of his wife; but it is particularly difficult if that proud woman is also a proud black. In 1973 Silvia found out about a job as an assistant to the United States Secretary of Health Education and Welfare. Obviously she was unqualified for the job and I told her so, asking her why she thought she would have a chance.

"I am black and Spanish," she responded instantaneously. "They need blacks and Spanish people these days."

As the conversation progressed, emotions increased. As a friend of mine said to me later, the practical thing for me to do would have been to keep quiet and let her apply and find out for herself she was underqualified. But in an effort to prevent my spouse from exerting her energy in applying for a job she could not get, I had made a mistake — a mistake that produced emotion-packed differences between us only because there was an ethnic difference between us.

I said in my closing statement at the 1973 marriage encounter — such as each participant was asked to make to the group — that although Silvia and I had come to the encounter with doubts, our seeing that we were not the only couple whose marriage was a little less perfect than we had once envisioned it made us less apprehensive about what very few imperfections existed in our relationship, and more thankful about the very many perfections that existed in it.

Our relationsip did improve for about a month, but then we again began having frequent arguments about a wide variety of subjects. Race or culture became a part of almost every argument regardless of the initial subject. By now I had called Silvia a nigger once or twice, something I would have considered inconceivable two or three years earlier. A number of times I had termed her requests for increased family expenditures as efforts to keep up with the black nouveau riche.

When I frequently disagreed with her about any of a wide variety of subjects, she frequently told me my ideas were very

127

middle class, very white middle class, or very small town middle class. American society has now labeled nigger or any other ethnic phrase a no-no word, so she had no trouble in supporting her condemnation of me for saying nigger. But since our society is white middle class, it is usually considered more of a compliment than an insult to be told you are thinking in the vane of a white middle class person. Yet it was precisely because I had tried to foresake my white middle class culture in favor of a black spouse, that it hurt deeply for her to term me white middle class. In doing that, she was classifying me as something I did not think I was: she was classifying me as part of a group from which she felt increasingly distant and for whose ideas she had increasingly little respect. She did not realize it, but it hurt as much for my black spouse to stereotype me as a "white" as it hurt her to have me stereotype her as a "black" or even a "nigger."

Ironically, one of the most divisive factors was that which should have been the most unifying, religion. Silvia had been elected to the Session — the ruling body — of our church. We were happy about this and enjoyed her having a leadership role there. I thought she was a little bit out of place and unprepared when on Layman's Sunday in 1972 she spent much of her ten-minute sermonette telling the all-white congregation about how she felt as a black person, but I didn't mind that.

I did mind when the following year she started criticizing to me the philosophy of certain members of the congregation, and also when she told me how disgusted she was with the Session. Since then I have served on the Session and can appreciate her frustration, but at the time it seemed to me that she was running down the church and its members; and I identified with them if for no other reason that that they were my color. In public I spoke out against their politics, economic theories, and racial attitudes more than she, and I often did the same at home. But it was O.K. for me to criticize my fellow whites, publicly and privately; it was *not* O.K. for her to exercise the same privilege. It apparently was the same thing that happened when blacks were involved: she would criticize them, but often did not like it when I criticized them. This was particularly evident in regard to the blacks with whom she dealt at work: she could tell me her criticism of a black one night, but would become angered when I, the next week, made a similar reference to the same person based on Silvia's previous comments to me.

When Silvia became less active in the church in 1973 as she became more active in her job, I looked upon this as a disinterest in a white church, not a disinterest in a church. Her increasing tendency to see everything in a racial context was evident in one ride home from a Sunday morning service in late 1973. As usual we were discussing the minister's sermon. He had made a quick and innocent reference to the common phrase "this is not a black and white issue," referring to a situation in which there was no clear-cut indication as to what was right and what was wrong. Silvia said his use of this phrase showed that the minister was insensitive to the racial connotation.

When I answered that the phrase was a common one and that it was ridiculous to attach it to the user's racial philosophy, she replied: "It doesn't make any difference if it's a common phrase. Blacks can regard that as demeaning. The whole implication is that white is good and black is the opposite of good."

My most disgraceful action involving Silvia and me and the church was related to my greatest accomplishment in the church. Early in 1973, realizing that no young adults were attending Sunday school, I organized a class. By preparing good lessons and, with Silvia's help, contacting all the potential members in this very small church, I built the class up to about ten regular members. Silvia told me I was doing an excellent job, and at first enjoyed going. Then, as she began to feel alienated from the philosophy and social outlook of the class members, she began attending less regularly. I complained loudly to her, saying that if I spent three hours preparing the lesson, she could take twenty minutes to read it and one hour to attend the class. One Saturday night when she said she had something else to do beside read the lesson, and indicated that she was not going to attend the next morning, my emotions burned as I sat in the living room preparing the lesson. I asked her when she was going to read her lesson. No response. "Are you going to class tomorrow?" I asked.

"If I have the time," she responded, somewhat disinterested, somewhat defiant.

I went into the bedroom, saw the book about black culture she was reading, grabbed it out of her hand and hit her with the Bible I had in my hand.

She complained. I felt miserable. I tried to explain that I felt like a hypocrite hitting her with the Bible, but also felt like a hypocrite asking other people to attend the class when my own wife did not even think it was worth attending.

Needless to say, I am not proud of this incident. Obviously the Bible is not to be used to hit people; obviously hitting people is not the way to attract them to Sunday School. I feel that it is important to focus on this incident, however — even though it would not occur in most marriages, biracial or otherwise — because it illustrates the extent to which Silvia's and my cultures were in conflict — or at least the extent to which we were in conflict and seemed to feel that our cultures were in conflict. I cannot prove, but I do know, that if that woman lying on that bed had been white, I would never have hit her. I would have been disgusted that she had found another book, whether textbook, novel, or otherwise, more important than the Sunday School lesson I was studying. But I would have realized that I was disgusted with but an individual whose disinterest in religion at that moment in history was not much different from the disinterest that most others in our culture, including myself, had experienced in recent years. But Silvia's case I regarded not as the weakness of a person within my own culture, but rather as the weakness of the product of another culture. I stood not as one human battling the weaknesses of another human, but as one human facing the product of another culture — a culture I did not understand and therefore was desperate as to how to combat.

I was looking forward to our holiday vacation that year in Iowa, even though I could tell that Silvia was not very excited. I thought that perhaps ten days of relaxation would put everybody in a better mood. She told me in 1975 that by the time of that trip she had made up her mind that we could not get along

130

without a marriage counselor, which I said we did not need. Seeing the generally happy family relationships among people in small-town America who had never heard of a marriage counselor convinced me all the more that we did not need a counselor.

We had gone as a family to several Christmas concerts in Miami, but they had been my idea and she went along more to avoid argument than to enjoy them. Anyway, when we went from work to the airport the Friday before Christmas, I felt good and continued to feel that way until we were off the runway and had shown Heather and Silvia the gifts I had gotten at my office party. Silvia was not nasty, just distant, further away than the 1300 miles between us and Iowa. Once we got to Clarksville, she was sulky and refused to do much of anything with me, even limiting her conversations with my mother to times when I wasn't around, such as when she was helping her wash the dishes. In Clarksville we were in four worlds: Pat with his family or local residents, Pat and Heather, Silvia by herself or with Heather, Silvia with my family or local residents. None of these worlds met. The more I enjoyed visiting with local residents, the more distant I felt from that wife of another culture. The more I had a good time sledding and making a snowman with Heather, the more distant I felt from Silvia, who refused our invitation to participate. The more Heather and I visited grandmother and great-aunt, the more distant I felt from the Silvia who had refused to make it a threesome as we had done on past visits. This became particularly hard for me when the great-aunt, the angel of the community as well as the family, and now dying of cancer, asked me on several visits where Silvia was and if she was all right. The more Silvia took Heather to grandmother's house when I wasn't around, the more left out I felt.

On earlier visits, I had been delighted by the way Silvia's dynamic personality and intelligence had led local residents not only to accept her, but to like her. This time, because of the way she told local residents about herself rather than about us, I felt she no longer was content with proving to the home-town folks she was Pat Huber's equal — she was out to show them she was his superior. I suspected the same goal, even

131

though the approach was more subtle, when she talked to my mother. This particularly infuriated me because I had spent ten years giving my parents a sales job on Silvia — telling them only the good parts about her. I had made sure my mother's opinion of her was not warped by letting her know about Silvia's relative who was on dope, or the one who had an illegitimate child. Now Silvia seemed to be using the confidence I had encouraged my mother to have in her to raise my mother's opinion of her even higher, while inducing her to have a lower opinion of her son.

I felt particularly far from Silvia — and I suppose she did from me — because I was in the homeland, a homeland which now meant more to me each time I returned to it. As I looked at the front of the clothing store where my family's name had been taken down earlier that year — symbolizing the end of the fifty-two years the business had been owned by my family — I could not help but wonder if maybe I should have continued the successful business as so many local residents had predicted I would do. When I was planning to marry Silvia Silva, I had told her I had no interest in the clothing business and did not plan to stay in Clarksville, and so therefore she did not have to be concerned about living in a small all-white town very different from anywhere she had ever lived. She nodded. I thought she was saying she was glad I planned to live in a more urban area, but wanted to live with me no matter where I was. But now I was thinking about her saying a year earlier that she definitely would not live in small-town Iowa, regardless of what I might want to do. Now that I was looking at the name of the firm which had purchased Huber's, I was forgetting my decision not to take over the business. I was remembering my wife's dictate that I could not purchase the business and remain, in effect, her husband.

When Silvia gave me the book *Open Marriage* for Christmas, I regarded it as another example of her insistence we had marital difficulties, a contention I was not ready to accept. Besides that, I was a little bit acquainted with the book and had already discussed it with her. Basically she, like the authors, said that each spouse is an individual living and working towards his
132

own satisfaction. I said that a married person is not an individual but one-half of a married unit. My position seemed particularly valid there in rural America, where marriage is regarded in the traditional manner.

Needless to say, it was not a Merry Christmas. And it was not a Happy New Year, for after several requests in early January to get me to go with her to a marriage counselor, she became convinced we could not live together happily, at least without a counselor. By mid-January she — unknown to me — had seen a lawyer. She set January 31 as the day to move out.

It was not a Happy New Year for Silvia or Pat, nor was it a happy time for Heather, who now was well aware that mom and dad had arguments. She was also well aware that mom and dad were not the same color.

CHAPTER VIII

Color Through The Child's Eyes

"I don't want to be white," Heather suddenly announced loudly as she stood in front of her parents on a fall evening in 1971. "I don't want to be white because white people are diabetics and I don't want to be a diabetic."

Unable to pronounce the word clearly, making it sound more like "diatetic" than "diabetic", this three and one-half-year-old had been able to make a connection: dad was white and he was a diabetic.

"I want to be black because black people don't have diatetics — black people don't have diabetes."

When Silvia and I tried to explain that this was not the case, she defended her theory: dad was white and he was a diabetic; mom was black and she did not have diabetes. Therefore, all whites have diabetes and no blacks have it.

Until two weeks earlier, Heather had never mentioned the skin color of her parents or anyone else. Silvia and I had noticed her apparently complete indifference to skin color. It had been particularly noticeable because this youngster, blessed with near-genious intelligence, was very observant of other differences between mom and dad, sexual and otherwise. Her playmates, all of whom were white, were distinguished as male and female and as good and bad, but their color was not mentioned.

The biggest distinction she had made among her playmates occured one day when she came running into the house excitedly to inform us: "Sammy has a tail." She then went on to explain that he had invited her to see him in the nude. After Silvia and I told Heather not to accept invitations to such exhibits, we joked with each other that if the exhibitor had been black and the audience white, every mother on the block would probably have heard about it within two days.

Although Silvia and I did not mention skin color to Heather, others did and she did not respond. When my mother gave her granddaughter a bath in early 1973, she was enough intrigued by this different experience to ask Heather: "How do you tell when you are clean?"

Heather stopped squirming around in the tub, looked at her grandmother a moment, didn't see any sense in the question, and went back to splashing in the water.

Now the recognition of color difference was coming all at once. Physical differences between mother and dad, earlier attributed to one being man and the other woman, were now attributed to one of us being white and the other black. Everything else about us was now also attached to our color difference. When she needed something done that required strength, she went to dad because "he is strong since he is white." Mother went to work every day "because she is black, but dad stays home because he is white."

In his first letter to us after the birth of Heather, my father pointed out the name we had given his grandchild was a long-standing term used in his business, the clothing industry, to refer to a "blend of colors." By her fourth birthday in January, 1972, Heather was not willing to consider herself a blending of colors: it had to be one or the other. "What color am I, black or white?" she asked frequently. We explained openly that she was neither black nor white, but brown. At first it bothered her when other children asked her what color she was, but by mid-1972 she enjoyed the question. It gave her a chance to show off by going into an authoritative dissertation as to why she was neither black nor white, like her parents, but somewhere in between, because she had part of each of us in her. By late 1972 color was not a problem for her: she understood why she was like neither parent and had little contact with youngsters or adults who demeaned those who had black or brown skins. She was bothered when a boy at nursery school, with whom she enjoyed both playing and fighting, told her his

135

dad would cut off her head because she was black. Once Silvia told Heather this was not the case, that her favorite friend and enemy was just trying to scare her, Heather was no longer bothered.

Also when she was four, Heather said she liked to visit my mother better than Silvia's mother because my mother was white and so had a nicer house. This concern couldn't be answered sociologically, for in fact the average white does have a better house than the average black. But no problem resulted. Thanks to our lying to her a little bit and also pointing out the middle class houses of our and Heather's black acquaintances, Heather was shown that blacks have nice houses just as do whites.

As Heather became aware during 1972 that her parents' other differences were not the result of color differences, she schemed with increasing frequency to tell us our actions resulted from our skin color. If mother disciplined her, mother was mean because she was black: "I like white people because they are nice, but I don't like blacks because they are mean." The reverse was said when dad disciplined her. At this age it was usually easy to deny that skin color had anything to do with our respective actions. In fact, we were humored by her tactics. Within a couple years, however, the schemes became more subtle, harder for the parents to combat, and caused more division between the parents.

Heather used the racial "gimmick" to its utmost in February, 1975. An aggressive, domineering, and often hot tempered youngster, she was disciplined one day at school for hitting other youngsters. Her explanation: "They called me nigger and they wouldn't stop." Crying loudly in her astute melodramatic fashion, she continued by whining: "They keep calling me nigger and the teacher doesn't do anything about it. I ask them to stop and they won't stop."

When I asked why she didn't ask the teacher to stop the other youngsters, she cried some more: "I ask the teacher and she doesn't do anything. She doesn't even care."

By this time she had her mother's sympathy. Her mother criticized me for suggesting that the teacher might be of help,

136

saying she herself had already talked to the teacher about it. When I started to tell Heather that no matter what the youngsters said, it did not justify hitting them, Silvia jerked her head toward me and commanded me to be quiet.

"Quit scolding her. She is upset by this. I have talked to the teacher about this. I am going to school tomorrow morning to tell the principal that the teacher has to stop those kids."

Having been put in my place, I withdrew from the argument, but not without telling Silvia that Heather's excuse for this misbehavior was no more legitimate than the non-racial excuses she had given for the several other incidents in which she had been involved that school year.

Heather saw she had a real "winner" in that racial excuse she had given. Her mistake was overplaying her hand and losing the whole jackpot. For about a week, her misbehavior of each day was attributed to her being black, everything from talking in class to throwing sand at another youngster.

The first night after the argument, I was afraid to mention the subject to Silvia, but she mentioned it to Heather, telling her that if she were bothered by what somebody said, just to ignore them. The following night she told me she was convinced Heather was using the racial angle as an excuse, even though she might have been a little bothered. Heather's scheme became more obvious the next week when she tried to defend writing on the school's bathroom walls by saying that if she didn't write on them, somebody would write something there that was bad about black people. When I asked if anybody had written anything there against black people, she said: "Well, no. . . but they might."

Heather's use of her biracialness as a device showed that she was not much bothered by it. Indeed, in her fourth, fifth, and sixth years, she mentioned it only once every five or six days, rather than talking about it continuously as she had during the first few months following her first mention of it. Most of the time she did mention it came as the result of what few racist remarks other children made to her. When the remarks were made, she met the challenge because of her overall self-confidence, cockiness, above average intelligence, and tough behavior. When she was confronted with racist remarks, she tended to go only to her black parent to discuss the matter, but the problem of racism for her as a "half black" was not much different from that for a total black. The challenge unique to her or to any other interracial youngster is that of identity. After those first few months when she asked "Who am I?" she seemed to overcome this problem, dealing with it in a variety of ways.

When she was four and she and I were playing at a public playground while her mother rested back in the car, I pushed her around a merry-go-round along with several other youngsters, all white. After a brief ride, the oldest in the group, a girl probably six or seven, asked me if I was with "that girl." I answered yes. She asked why I was with her. I said because she was my daughter. I sensed what she had noticed, but not wanting to ruin an unplanned opportunity to study child psychology, I did not elaborate, wanting to let the girl do the talking. She didn't talk.

A couple rides later, she came up to me again and said: "Did you say that was your daughter?" After I answered yes, she looked at Heather again, still puzzled, shook her head and turned to me to say: "She sure must go to the beach a lot."

Heather heard the entire conversation and said nothing, well aware that she looked different than either of her parents — but apparently completely unbothered by it, and not even interested in explaining it to the girl. She had already had a good time repeating numerous times her dissertation about how she was not the same color as either of us, and she didn't want to bother with that again.

This contrasts with her attitude two years later in 1974, when she and I were flying a kite on a Sunday afternoon in March. This was after Silvia had moved away from the house, and so she wasn't around. Heather and I were at a playground of a predominantly white school in a totally white residential area near our own, so the ten or twelve children flying kites at the same time were all white. As Heather and I were making one of our numerous efforts to unravel our kite string, a girl who looked about ten or twelve years old volunteered to give us a hand. After the string was unravelled, we got the kite back in the air, largely because of her help.

Then the brisk March wind caused us some more problems, the string was tangled again, and we were grounded. The same girl came to us again, started to help some more and then realized the knots in our string were hopeless. She looked at us more than at the knots. She asked politely but inquisitively: "Is that your daughter?"

I said yes. Heather, who was facing in the other direction as she continued to work with the string, turned when the question was asked, but then turned back without saying anything. The older girl added: "She certainly doesn't look very much like you." She then walked over to Heather and said, perplexed, somewhat like the girl on the merry-go-round two years earlier: "Is that your father?"

Heather responded quickly: "Yes." Realizing the girl's problem in believing her skin came from me, she stated in a matter-of-fact manner: "I look more like my mother than I look like my dad."

This did not shock me. She was just verbalizing what I knew already to be so: Heather regarded herself as part of each of us, but more a part of her mother than a part of me. It is hard to tell what factors played a role in her feeling this way. Probably it had something to do with the black parent being the same sex. Probably she felt that she belonged to a minority group, and leaned toward the parent who also belonged to one.

The belief not only in the tendency but perhaps the desirability that the biracial youngster take this course is presented in *Interracial Marriage: Expectations and Realities* by Irving R. Stuart and Lawrence E. Abt (Grossman Publishers, 1973). This book presents an example of a middle class black father telling his wife that their daughter is black. The white wife rebelled, saying that the youngster was the equal product of each of them. The father countered by pointing out that a biracial person is categorized as black by society, and therefore their daughter should be prepared to recognize her blackness.

Quoting this example in a paper for an education psychology course later in 1974, Silvia wrote: "Thus we have a situation in

139

which both parents give logical explanations for their opinions. If the father's side is taken, how can the daughter regard her mother as equal to her father? If the mother's side is taken, will the daughter be able to make the psychological adjustment to the fact that in spite of what her parents tell her, the world says she is black?"

A TV comedy program in early 1975 focused upon the atmosphere in a Negro family the evening before the two teenage boys were to be bused for the first time to a predominantly white school. Humorously treating the reassurance one apprehensive boy was attempting to give his brother that night as they tried to go to sleep, the script had the boy say haltingly: "Going to school with white kids is nothing to worry about."

Heather, in the room by herself, blurted out: "Oh yes it is."

"They'll treat black kids just like anybody else," the boy on TV continued.

"That's what you think!" Heather corrected him, speaking not from fear but with definiteness.

It seemed clear Heather had answered without difficulty the question of "Who am I" by saying "I am part of each. I am more like the black parent and have the same problems as blacks. But most of all, I'm not concerned about skin color because that is something my parents have told me not to worry about."

Heather, whose name meant "a blend of colors" in the clothing industry, had seemed to have had less trouble deciding how she was blended than had her parents. Either in the early 1970's Silvia and I had lost that acceptance of a blend of colors we had envisioned in the 1960's, or we had never really made that acceptance in spite of thinking we had.

Many people say their primary reservation about interracial marriages is the problems resulting from interracial children. My mother reflected a common attitude when she told me a year before my marriage that special consideration should be given to the problems of biracial children, "since they have the problems of both races." The concern was evident in the *New York Times* story we had read in October, 1963, in which even though all the couples interviewed termed their interracial

140

marriages successful, several expressed hesitancy about having interracial children. Silvia and I did not ignore the subject during our courtship. We just could not conceive of its being a problem.

When we did think about a biracial child, we were thinking of a concept, not a real live human being. Our theories about interracial children were sincere. We could see no significant problem in having biracial children, and saw numerous advantages in their being biracial, since that would give them an identity with people of two races and two cultures, not just one. The advantages were logical and were easy to agree upon — as long as we were talking in the abstract. They were easy to agree upon as long as the child was a babe-in-arms, a time when she was truly regarded by Silvia and me as the blending of our colors, our cultures, our personalities. We were particularly proud of her because we considered her a blend of us. Biracial Heather was not a true blend of colors when she was an infant, however, because she cried for her bottle, wet her diapers, toddled around, and learned to talk in the same way as would a baby of all-white or all-black parentage. Her color, culture, and personality were submerged, not blended. Our willingness to accept her as a blend of us would not be tested until after her third birthday.

At her third birthday party, I couldn't help notice that Silvia had invited several of Heather's friends living a considerable distance away, all of them black, rather than limit it to her friends in the neighborhood, a neighborhood that was completely white. Several weeks later, Silvia stated: "I am bothered that Heather doesn't have any black youngsters to play with in this neighborhood. She needs to play with youngsters like herself."

I rebelled hotly, resenting Silvia's announcement that Heather was black. I was more bothered that she attached any significance to the color of Heather's playmates. "That doesn't make any difference. She gets along O.K. with the kids around here she always plays with," I replied. "Why do you say she needs somebody black to play with? She is not black — she's brown. Don't forget she has got some of my genes in her."

141

"She's black," Silvia corrected me. "Studies show that a biracial child considers himself black. Anybody that has had any sociology knows that."

Infuriated by this stupid idea and by her supporting it with a reference to sociology, since I knew sociologists presented this type of absurd idea in order to stay in business, I was concerned that Silvia attached so much importance to the color of Heather's playmates. To me that was racism in reverse. Certainly I would never tell an all-white child of mine to play with more whites and fewer blacks. Now however, my wife was saying her child should play with blacks rather than with so many whites.

Silvia's statement that Heather was black haunted me for months. It was in my mind when Silvia started saying in 1971 that Heather needed some books that had more pictures of black people in them than did the ones she had. At first I politely ignored her statements, but finally I got tired of them and said that Heather had plenty of books as it was; and since they certainly weren't racist, Silvia was making a big deal out of nothing. She showed her respect for my opinion by buying several black childrens' books the next week. She also complained to the public library about their not being enough black childrens' books — although there were some. This action I admired more than criticized because there was an obvious need for it, a need I had recognized since my high school days. But while admiring Silvia's action of getting more books for black children, I resented her thinking that my youngster was black.

Our definiteness about each of us considering Heather to be our respective color was shown clearly by an incident soon after we moved into our house in 1972. Silvia mentioned that the school three blocks away, which Heather would be eligible to attend in two years, might be one of the first in Dade County to participate in a limited school busing program for school integration. I said I was glad to hear that, and that I thought we should make sure Heather was among those bused in order to increase by one the usually small minority of parents volunteering to have their children participate in such projects. I waited for Silvia to say: "Yes. I think that would be a worthwhile way to do our small part."

That's not what she said. She declared loudly, authoritatively, almost defiantly: "They aren't going to bus her. I don't want my daughter bused."

Trying to clear my mind quickly, I reviewed my thoughts to make sure I was not talking to an anti-integrationist mother imagining the big bad things that were going to happen to her child if bused to a predominantly black school. Knowing that Silvia and I favored school busing, I asked: "Why do you say that? Somebody has to let their child be bused."

"I am not going to have Heather taking an hour-long bus ride when there is a school just three blocks away. They can bus some white kids."

Finally the truth came out. I thought Heather was white and so should be bused. Silvia, although having the opposition to long bus rides for her child that most mothers seem to have, was against her daughter being bused primarily because she considered her black.

There was one time Heather was indeed black. That was in the summer of 1973 when she was enrolled in a program in which the participants spent most of their time out of doors. Like many whites, I used to think a black's color is uninfluenced by the sun, but by then I had been married long enough to know differently. Heather got so much sun that summer she became almost as black as her mother. This amused all three of us; and I joked that we would have to send her back north to give her white skin a chance to show itself.

There were other times when Heather's skin color was the subject of light conversation among us. She kind of liked it when I told her that her rear-end must have been one of the parts of her body she got from me, since it was lighter colored than the rest of her. And she enjoyed challenging comments I made once or twice that she needed to take a bath because she was brown all over. And even though I resented Silvia's insisting in 1972 that Heather needed some black dolls, she had a good time taking care of the one black and one white doll she had by 1974. It was a little heartwarming to see her have her white doll and her black doll put to bed side by side under the same blanket. Silvia and I enjoyed talking about how Heather referred
143

to the dolls by the names she had given them, not by their colors. When I asked which was which, she told me not in terms of their color but by referring to their relative positions in relation to the wall near where they slept.

Heather's black and white dolls symbolized the ease with which she dealt with both races. Indeed, our pre-marriage speculation that an interracial child would or could have a close identity to two races rather than to just one had proven to be the case in actual practice as well as in theory. Heather was not ignorant of the differences between peoples' colors — just not bothered by them. She was not bothered much by the differences between Cubans and Anglos, either, although she was more conscious of it, presumably because of the language differences.

During her first three years, the parental decisions involving Heather, as with most children, were simple. Arguments occured, but they involved primarily mechanical things such as who was going to feed her and when it was time to buy a bed for her. After that, the parental decisions became more complex and there was more opportunity for disagreement. And as the decisions became less ones of mechanics and more ones of judgement and philosophy, disagreements about Heather became more likely to have ethnic connotations, even where there was no basis for it.

Example 1: Silvia, like many mothers, wants to take child to doctor more often than necessary. Pat, like many fathers, wants to de-emphasize children's illnesses and injuries, sometimes to too great an extent. Rather than leave this as a common mother-father disagreement, Silvia says it shows my German coldness for human welfare, and I say it shows her Spanish preoccupation with children.

Example 2: Silvia, like many mothers, wanted her daughter to take piano lessons at about age four. I, like many fathers, concerned about the cost in relation to what a four-year-old can learn, said I wanted her to take lessons but thought she should wait a year or two. Ultimately I accused Silvia of wanting to have her child do what upper middle class children do so that she could show off her black child. She said I was so

144

tight, so Scotch, that I was blinded to human and artistic values.

Example 3: Because of my diabetic diet and rural heritage, I was convinced that Heather should have a glass of milk at every meal. Silvia said this was not necessary, that my thinking was old fashioned and small townish. I said she didn't know the value of milk because she had grown up in a slum where people didn't have the money or the brains to drink it regularly.

Example 4: Silvia says I don't know anything about raising children because I was an only child and because I had not read any books about it. I say that the size of a family is not directly proportionate to ones knowledge of raising children: in fact, the best parents are those who have sense enough not to have a big family.

Tom Healey, my friend from work, asked as soon as I told him about Silvia's divorce suit: "Tell me! Is Heather part of the problem?" Although he had seen her but once, his insight had enabled him to see that "she is a very strong-willed person and might cause friction between you." He saw this even though Heather's parents had not. In retrospect here is what happened:

Because we had encouraged her to look at things thoughtfully and questioningly, and because she was intelligent, Heather was not content to accept something simply because mother or dad said it was so: she wanted us to explain our decisions. Explanations of decisions often reveal differences in viewpoints. Differences in viewpoints lead to arguments. We found with increasing frequency in 1973 that we attributed our different viewpoints to our different colors, or to our different childhoods.

Heather's accomplishments as well as her problems were occasionally viewed by her parents, or at least by me, in terms of race — even though there was no racial basis for them. Like most fathers, I had not been as interested as mother in the baby or the two- or three-year-old. I had not cared if she was more black than white when her big achievements were looking pretty in a picture or saying cute words, because these "achievements" were unimportant anyway as far as I was concerned. But when she was in first and second grades bringing home

145

report cards with A's on them, playing in a piano recital, singing in the church choir, telling people about what she had learned from her extensive reading, I knew the events were important and so wanted to be at least half her parent.

But by that time I had let myself become the secondary parent. As a child progresses beyond his first three or four years, many fathers try to re-establish themselves as equal partners in parenthood. I felt the job a little harder because while I was making up for not having changed as many diapers as mom — or read as many books to Heather — I also had to combat the fact that she now considered herself closer to the color of her mother than to that of me. Her definiteness about her color was beyond question by her sixth birthday. That is shown clearly, even though humorously, by an event shortly before her seventh birthday when the three of us were watching television coverage of a women's amateur track meet.

"I am for that one," Heather announced as the competitors in the 880 yard race broke from the starting blocks. "Come on! Beat them!" she yelled at the top of her voice as they rounded the first turn.

"Which one are you for?" I asked innocently, knowing the answer to my question.

She was too busy cheering to answer me, so I repeated my question a minute later. As they turned into the final straight away, she pointed to the one black woman in the race, increasing the volume of her yells with that of the crowd as the runners approached the finish line, and Heather's favorite won.

"Oh thank goodness," Heather sighed, almost exhausted. "I was so worried."

"Why were you for that woman?" I asked. "Had you seen her run before?"

"No. But she is black and I am black and so I am for her," she said, implying that it was kind of silly to ask the question.

Heather went through the kindergarten two times at her nursery school, but still was not old enough to attend first grade in the public school system. Reports from the nursery school director indicated that Heather was both too capable and too ornery to stay there the next year, so Silvia and I agreed that we should send her to a private school where she could attend first grade.

As we were trying to choose a private school, I suggested a Spanish school so she could learn early the language I had promised Silvia I would learn but had not learned. Silvia was very cool to the idea, giving vague reasons. Finally after visiting several non-Spanish private schools, we visited and decided to send her to a Cuban school where English was the primary language, but Spanish classes were conducted daily.

Ironically, Silvia who had had enough reservations about the Spanish culture to hesitate sending her daughter to a Cuban school, used her similarity in culture and language to carry on all of our dealings with faculty and administration at the school. I, who had heralded the theory of sending my daughter to a school founded in a culture completely different from my own, felt isolated from the school and occasionally from my daughter attending it. This isolation was climaxed in February, 1974, when I, in an effort to get Heather out of school early one day, was told by someone in the principal's office that I could not get her out. When I pointed out she was my daughter, another Cuban woman said briskly in broken English: "Only Mrs. Huber can take her out because she brought her here."

Maybe this woman wasn't nasty, but her Cuban accent made me feel all the more distant from that daughter and mother. Heather Huber now had estranged parents. Parents of different color and culture had been no big deal through the child's eyes, but in the eyes of the parents, that child who had seemed to symbolize that marriage that had been a beautiful blend of colors, now seemed to symbolize a blend that wouldn't mix.

147

CHAPTER IX

A Renewal In Spring

"I wanted to tell you I had been thinking about the plans we made to move back together [I gulped, realizing this might be the time she'd say she changed her mind] and I am very happy about it. I am very happy about it and I just called because I wanted you to know how happy I am."

"Naturally it's very good to hear that," I said, not doing a very good job of hiding my excitement from my boss, whose phone I had used to take Silvia's call. After adding: "Of course I'm looking forward to it too," I made the conversation short. That's typical of me. As I left the phone, I smiled. That is not typical of me. It particularly had not been typical during the three months we had been separated. That May 5th, 1974, I was even happier than I'd been two or three days earlier when Silvia had agreed to move back into our house the coming weekend. As Friday evening approached (May 8), our happiness continued to build.

Like most of my actions, my proposal to her, like my marriage proposal, was calculated and well planned. As Silvia and I lived apart, I recognized that the longer we lived apart the less likely it was that we would get back together. I saw her happiness as a separated woman serving to verify to her the idea she should be separated, and I saw her unhappiness as a separated woman encouraging her to go ahead and relieve herself of her estranged husband.

She had told me she had thought carefully about leaving before actually doing it, and was not going to make a quick decision to return. With this in mind, my strategy was to suggest

148

the first week in May that she return on a temporary basis. I said that neither she nor I could make the final decision as to whether we wanted to stay married until we lived together again for awhile. I said the longer we lived apart, the more used to it we would be, and so the less likely would be the chance of our being happy when we tried again to live together. I suggested that since Mother's Day was May 10, all three of us might have a happier Mother's Day if she and Heather returned that weekend. I quickly mentioned a Saturday night dance to which I would take her — a sign of my desperation, the opportunity to attend our church service together on Mother's Day, and then after that the opportunity to attend a special Mother's Day service to be conducted at the First Unitarian Church of Miami. I emphasized that her return would be only on a trial basis and that she could leave whenever she wanted. She hesitated only a moment and said yes.

I rode to Silvia's apartment that Friday evening with a church friend who had been concerned about our break-up and was very happy to lend me his trailer to pick up Heather's piano. Also along were two other friends of Silvia's and mine, equally glad to see us trying to rejoin each other. Even the economics of it appealed to me: here I was borrowing the trailer from a Scotch Presbyterian, whereas Silvia had hired someone to move the piano to her apartment several days after moving out, despite my appeals that that would be an unnecessary expenditure, an amount greater than I made in a day's work.

Not only was the piano being moved in instead of out, but everything was right out in the open — not only the piano and furniture, but also the terms under which Silvia and Heather were returning. The only trickery on my part was that once the piano was in the trailer, I told Silvia that we might as well use the extra space in it by hauling whatever else she and Heather could get along without that night, pretending that I expected Heather and her to stay in the apartment until the next day, as scheduled. By the time we (including Silvia) brought the trailer back for a second load, Silvia, Heather, the driver, and the two helpers all realized that the two of them were going to move back in with me that night rather than wait until the next night, as scheduled.

After the second trailer load, we made several trips in our own car to pick up the rest of the things in Silvia's apartment. Heather worked hard at helping, showing by her concentration on the job and by her excitement that she was happy about the move. When we moved in the piano, we dropped it on its side, but I would be able to fix it on Saturday. There was music in the air without piano or song or instruments.

The next heaviest items we moved were the twin beds which Silvia and Heather had been using. Heather, like Silvia and me, was so tired she did not need to be encouraged to go to bed after the move was completed. For Silvia and me, this was not a night for twin beds, but rather a return to that double bed in which we had not slept together for over three months. We had been careful throughout most of our marriage to engage in sexual intercourse only when it was the emotional expression of true love rather than a means of entertainment, a response to immediate emotions. I reminded Silvia of this and we decided that this occasion was too happy and too indicative of the true love between us, not to be climaxed with sex.

Saturday wasn't that sexy, but just as romantic, as we cleaned up the house, moved things around, and did so much work that we were tired by 7 P.M. So tired, in fact, that we decided not to go to the dance, even though we had both looked forward to it. Although we had both regarded the dance as a confirmation of our desire to try to get back together, we found this desire reflected even better in worship Sunday morning. Helpful was a friendly greeting from numerous members of our small church. And realizing that despite the necessity of the spiritual and the intellectual, it is sometimes valuable to have a few of those niceties I had always assumed my marital relationship too strong to need, I had gotten corsages for Silvia and Heather that Mother's Day — the first time I had done it. This added to the nice aroma of their return.

"My mother and daddy moved back together to see if they could live with each other without arguing and fighting," Heather told a friend about three weeks later, "and they are doing a very very good job."

150

When I recited this to my mother over the phone a night or two later, she restrained her emotions as she always does, but I could tell her happiness at the change in a situation that had been a very unhappy one for her. "Well, " she said of Heather's comment, "sometimes from the mouths of babes. . ." I don't think she said "gems," but she and I, and Silvia and Heather all recognized the gem. A week later when I reminded Silvia that she had been back a month and wondered if she was going to move out now that the month's trial period was over, neither of us needed the other to tell him that her moving back out seemed almost ridiculous.

About this time we hired a maid, something I had agreed to do soon after her return, realizing that my complaint of a year ago about the cost of a maid seemed trivial when compared to the cost of living separately and divorcing each other. Now that I had told Silvia to hire one, I wondered why it took her so long. I was puzzled by her reaction when I said we should discriminate in reverse and find a black maid. "After all, when your job is getting jobs for blacks, we should hire one when we have the opportunity," I told her. She looked at it differently. I thought it would be giving a black a break to hire her; Silvia did not. Her job was to get good jobs for blacks, not the traditional service or clerical job. I wondered if that was what she was thinking when she responded to my suggestion by saying: "It is hard to find a black maid. Black maids don't like to work for blacks."

Anyway, by late June she had gotten a maid, a black; and we both were glad — Silvia because she did not have as much housework to do, and I because the housework got done. "It's nice to come home to a clean house," Silvia said during the evening after the maid's second or third visit. Silvia, when referring to the maid in Heather's presence, called her Mrs.____, not "the maid," and told me to do likewise. I didn't appreciate the importance of it. In fact a few times when I was mad at my black wife, I made sure I referred to the maid as such, just to let my black wife know that I didn't give special treatment to people just because they were black.

The maid soon had some new furniture to dust, about

$1,000-worth of it replacing the junk we had had in our living room. Here again this was an admission on my part that a few nice physical surroundings were not extravagance, but rather gave husband and wife a little better atmosphere in which to get along. I had proposed buying the furniture several months before Silvia left, but had decided that we should wait until our financial situation improved in view of the decline in the stock we had bought.

We got the furniture at just above wholesale, a privilege granted by my employer to employees buying from any of the 100 furniture stores it owned. It boosted my ego to think that for once we were benefiting from *my* employer, after the free tuition and all the other benefits we had gotten from Silvia's employer. Our primary thought about the discount matter, however, was how to receive it without letting the store, and thus possibly my supervisors, know that my wife was black. One approach I suggested was to have me pick it out without Silvia's help, but we agreed that that was not desirable. Therefore we had fun working up a little scheme. We visited one of the firm's stores near our home without my identifying myself as an Aristar employee, getting the stock numbers of those pieces we might want to buy. Then Silvia visited a store the firm owned in downtown Miami, posing as a regular customer. She called me up at work that afternoon, telling me the stock numbers and location in the store of the pieces she thought we should purchase, adding she was calling me at work because they had told her the couch she liked was the last of its kind and so we should act quickly. I went to the store after work that evening, picked out the furniture, and bought it as an employee.

All this sounds a little involved merely to buy a piece of furniture in the United States in the 1970's; but Silvia and I had heard enough at various Miami businesses and from enough Miami friends to know that our tactics were not a matter of running from a paper tiger. The afternoon the furniture arrived, Heather, who had never seen her parents buy anything for more than $100, called me at work and said: "Daddy — you should see our new furniture. It is beautiful. It is the most beautifulest
152

furniture in the world."

Three weeks later we were buying another couch and other furniture for our Florida room. This time we went back to our neighborhood store, this time as white man and black wife, and identified ourselves properly as Aristar employees. The difference was that I was to be an employee but for another week — so I had just been told — and so wanted to take advantage of the discount before I became a former employee. Although we had not planned to refurnish the Florida room for at least another year, I decided that we should take advantage of the discount when we could.

Naturally, getting fired was no cause for joy. I couldn't help but wonder if a little bit of the reason was the bad mood I'd been in at work — as well as elsewhere — during the first four months of 1974 because of my marital problems. This thought tempted me to be angry at Silvia, particularly when viewed alongside the success she apparently had had in keeping her big smile at work during 1974, even though she was not always happy off the job. I controlled this resentment, however, because there was no point in it. Besides, I knew the primary reason for my dismissal was the serious financial condition at Aristar, a situation which would lead to the departure of its president, a vice president, the comptroller, and several lower level people in the financial department within six months.

The primary characteristic about my dismissal, so far as my relationship with Silvia was concerned, was our lack of panic, her confidence I could find something else, and my confidence that she meant what she said. I said to her: "I am sorry that soon after I find my wife, I lose my job. But I now know that I am a lot better off with my wife and without a job, than with a job and without my wife." She smiled as she spoke the last three or four words with me, knowing what I was going to say before I said it.

Polly Cook nodded understandingly when I told her this same thing a few nights later at a marriage counseling session. Polly, Director of the Wesley Foundation (Methodist) at the University of Miami, had counseled us from early May until our reunification, and saw us four or five times during the next six

153

months. Polly had been my last hope for getting together with Silvia. I asked her to counsel us not merely because I admired her, but because Silvia respected her. I would have gone to about anybody at that time; and Silvia appeared to want to go to almost no one to talk about our marriage. Polly was white, so that didn't help; but Silvia knew that her racial views were liberal. More important than the difference in race was the similarity in their views about women. Polly, because she was a professional woman, embodied much of what Silvia wanted to make sure she was allowed to be. Silvia knew that although Polly was no bra burner, she wanted society to give women equal rights and consider them capable of something besides motherhood. They were serving together on the Women's Commission at the University of Miami and this had brought out the similarity of their viewpoints. In spite of all this, Silvia was not very interested in our going to Polly. Her attitude appeared to be "O.K. — if you are still going to go on trying to get a counselor to re-unite us, I'll see her."

During our separation, I had played to Silvia's blackness as well as to her feminism, trying to get us back together. I began back in February at the dedication of an extensive new ten-story building completed by the Greater Miami YWCA while Silvia was serving on its board of directors. Before we were separated I gradually had been decreasing my praise of Silvia's YWCA work, beginning to resent the time she spent away from her family while trying to help other people solve their problems. I became suspicious that all she was interested in about the YWCA was its strong policy against racism. Now that I was trying in February to get her back, however, I not only went to the YWCA dedication and praised womanhood, but made an effort to speak in a very friendly manner to the black employees as we visited around the building.

And during our separation I thought a lot about the effect our color differences would have on her. Each of us spent a little more time during that period with members of our own race; and Silvia spent more time with a Puerto Rican friend of hers. I was afraid this commradship she was having with blacks and Spanish speaking people would make her wonder if she had not been losing a lot by not associating more with her own culture, instead of dividing her attention between her culture and that of her husband. My fear of her thinking this way was increased by my thinking this way as my association with my own culture increased during our separation.

Now that we were back together and seeing Polly in the last week of June, 1974, we were not thinking of the white one separated from the black one, but rather about my being separated from a green paycheck. We stated, and Polly agreed, that we did not want to let my unemployment reestablish my jealousy and our tension of the sort that had contributed to our problems in the first place. Polly saw, and we were convinced, that this was not going to be the case. We now had the spirit we had in the 1960's.

In several days Silvia arranged for me to talk with Dr. Henry King Stanford, president of the University of Miami, to see if he might know of any appropriate jobs anywhere in the area. Before his interview of me, I realized his seeing me was not a favor he could extend to everybody: obviously I was going to see him only because Silvia had asked him for the favor. It reminded me of some of the other benefits I had gotten through Silvia's work at the university, benefits I appreciated but which made me feel inferior to her. More important than any of this, however, was that her getting me this interview reflected our spirit of the 'sixties. As it turned out, the interview was not needed anyway: within ten days I got a slightly higher-paying job; and Silvia stated her pride in me — a statement that sounded like the one she had made in 1966 when, after being fired from *The Newark Advocate*, I got a better job within two weeks.

I approached with enthusiasm the new job, which was with a public agency. The situation was the exact opposite of Aristar — very relaxed, predominantly young staff, overpaid employees, majority of employees with college degrees, and after-supper staff parties at which a black spouse was an interesting curiosity — certainly not a liability, and perhaps even an asset. As far as the work was concerned, Silvia had told me that my job might not be so much a matter of keeping accurate financial records as making the financial records look good to the appropriate

155

public officials. Never having worked for a government agency, I didn't take her very seriously, thinking that her comments might be based on just a few experiences with bureaucrats — probably black bureaucrats at that.

During September, Silvia called me at work to say that a friend of hers had said Eastern Air Lines stock was a real bargain at 4 3/4. I made my usual effort to play the authority on financial matters, saying that Eastern had been having all kinds of trouble, was losing money in the current year, and faced the same gloomy prospects as most air lines now that their big profit years of the 1960's were past. She was not convinced with my knowledge as she had been when I had bought stock two years earlier. After I recommended against purchase, she went ahead and called Merrill Lynch and then called me back. She wasn't hostile to me, she just told me she wanted to go ahead and buy some. She did. She was not the same investor who had gone into a broker's office for the first time two years earlier to make a payment on our account. Silvia had said at that time that the receptionist looked a little puzzled when she walked in, perhaps ready to say: "Excuse me ma'm, but are you sure you are in the right building?"

Since that time in 1973, Silvia had heard a number of blacks talk about stocks. Besides that, she earned most of the money in our family, so presumably she had a right to say how part of it was invested. She only bought 100 shares of Eastern at 4 5/8, but we enjoyed watching it fluctuate above and below that level during the next few months. We often joked, sometimes needled, about the fact that even if her investment decision didn't make any money for us, it could not lose us as much as mine had.

About this same time she called me at work about a very different matter — a call she had received from New York saying that her sister, Hilda, was very upset because her husband had been arrested, and that Hilda wanted to come to stay with us. Silvia said she did not know what to do, but thought she should try to help in some way or other. Realizing Silvia's shock, I talked with her about it for fifteen minutes, expressing my concern and recognition of the problem while trying to help her keep it in proportion. I asked her about the various actions available to Hilda and to her, and urged that if she thought Hilda should come down to be with us, to do whatever possible to help her get here.

That night Silvia thanked me for my patience and understanding in talking to her when I saw she needed it, and for the analytical way in which I helped her examine the alternative courses to take. This was another example of my sincere desire to help others, including my encouragement of Hilda's visit to Newark and to Miami in 1971. Unfortunately, as in past instances, my idealistic desire to help someone of another culture was not followed by an adequate ability to relate to them on a personal basis — just as it had not been on Hilda's earlier visits to us.

After helping Hilda relax a couple of weeks, I started trying to "convert" her to my way of thinking. I expected too much of her financially, particularly after I was fired from my job in October. In short, I contributed to her moving from our house to an apartment in Miami, and then to her moving back to New York.

As for the firing — it was the result of what Silvia had warned me about but which I had ignored — being too concerned about the production of accurate financial records as efficiently as possible. I thought my boss conceived of my job as being the production of financial records as politically expedient as possible.

Since the adverse economic situation in late 1974 seriously limited the available accounting jobs, I decided to apply for a teaching position in the public school system. Two jobs were available for journalism and English teachers at two junior high schools. I was not eligible for one because under a court ruling requiring integrated faculties at each school in the Dade County system, that job had to be filled by a black. I joked with Silvia that I should have been half elibigle for that job. The other job was for a white teacher at a school having a black principal, a man whom Silvia and I happened to have met at a black fraternity dance some two years earlier.

With fifteen hours of undergraduate courses in English and a masters degree from the best journalism school in the country, as well as a successful record in my amateur teaching efforts, I knew I could do an excellent job. I was even more convinced of this after seeing the work of the present teacher and the attitude other teachers in the school had toward their work.

I didn't get the job. I cursed the bureaucracy of big city schools. I criticized the state's great emphasis upon teachers having had education courses, even if they didn't know anything about that which they were to teach. These were my big gripes. There was another one: that principal who did not hire me. Usually you don't like the guy who tells you you can't have a job, particularly if he talks to you in the disinterested way that principal talked to me. But that potential employer was the same color as my wife, and a close friend of one of my wife's fellow black employees at the university. I did not blame the man because he was black, but I did blame the man *who* was black. This did not get me into an argument with my black wife, but she did indicate that she thought I should be regarding him more as that "damn" employer — and not so much as that "damn black" employer.

Shortly after that, I dealt with a black employer of a different sort. A friend of Silvia's, a black, told me that this person was a big talker, interested in no one except himself, and an Uncle Tom who had been interested in his black skin only when it could do such things as put him in the $20,000 salary bracket. I couldn't believe the man could be all that bad, so I trusted him, spending several days getting the information he needed to obtain federal assistance for a black-owned business for which I was supposed to be the accountant. Silvia didn't criticize me. She just warned me not to be sympathetic with this person, and trusting of him because he was a black, and said he had been discriminated against, and was asking nothing but a fair chance from the world. Subsequent events proved her suspicion to be justified. I had benefited from having a black wife to warn me about the trickery of some blacks, just as at times she has benefited from having a white husband to warn her about whites.

Most of my time during late October and early November was spent studying for the C.P.A. exam. After the final day of

158

the three day test, I looked forward to going with Heather and Silvia to a University of Miami football game. On our way from our car to the Orange Bowl, I walked ahead to buy the tickets, since the first quarter had already started. I got separated from them and ended up walking around the Orange Bowl two times trying to find them, finally giving up and buying a seat for myself in the end zone. I enjoyed the game, but was mad when we met each other afterwards at the car. That's beside the point. We had realized that this football game, only the third we had attended since our marriage, was a type of entertainment — non-intellectual, unsociological, and somewhat expensive as it was — that we needed to participate in as family once in a while, in order to have a little fun.

We ended up seeing three more University of Miami games that year. Better yet, we saw the best professional game in the Orange Bowl that season — the battle between Miami and Buffalo for first place in the Eastern Division of the American Football Conference. I rooted for Buffalo; but Heather yelled herself hoarse for Bob Griese and Larry Czonka and the other Dolphins about whom her classmates had told her. Silvia rooted for the home team too. I teased her about this because she had told me after seeing the appearance on an entertainment show of the number one black back in professional football — a guy by the name of Simpson — that he was really smart and humble and good looking, not just a good football player. I told her that her cheers for the Dolphins meant she was neglicting her man — maybe I said "boy."

Silvia combated the apparent contradiction by saying she wanted the best for O.J., but could not forget the Dolphins. Continuing the O.J. joke, I gave Silvia for Christmas a paperback biography of him, writing on the card that although I realized O.J. was the number one man in her life, I intended to be a good second: because I was number two, I, like Avis, would try harder.

Other than the O.J. book, I didn't give Silvia much for Christmas, but I had learned that a few gifts *are* needed to show love, even if they are bought with money earned by the receiver. Our Christmas, 1974, was simple and happy — just the opposite of the previous year. Of course we had the annual argument about how, when, and where to put up the Christmas tree; but that problem was quickly solved. Heather did not visit Santa Claus as she had the previous Christmas, but she was happier because her parents were happier. We did not take the tour of Christmas decorations in Miami and Coral Gables as we had in previous years because it had been cancelled due to the energy crisis; but despite the cutback in lighted bulbs, there was more light in our yuletide season. Because of my failing to find out the places and dates, we did not attend two concerts of religious Christmas music as we had in 1973; but our Christmas season was more spiritual.

And we were closer to my mother, even though she was 1300 miles farther away than she had been the previous Christmas. Besides that, she decided to come to Miami on December 28 to visit us. We all enjoyed the expressed purpose of her visit — attendance of the Orange Bowl Game between Alabama and Notre Dame on New Year's Night. We were proud to indicate to her — and she, on the other hand, was happy to see — that things were considerably different from what they had been when we saw her during the holidays a year earlier. Even *more* different, as a matter of fact, from what they had been when she had visited us during our separation in March, 1974.

And in addition to everything else, there was another optimistic development. I could pick my mother up at the airport this time because the Florida Department of Motor Vehicles had ruled in December that I could obtain a driver's license, which I immediately got. This represented the climax of an effort that I had been making since the first year of our marriage. The lawyer, chairman of the Business Law Department at the University of Miami, who had represented me in the matter during the preceding two years, had generously donated his time. It disturbed me at the time that it was Silvia — and not I — who made this arrangement between me and the lawyer possible; but now that I had actually *gotten* the license, I was not bothered at all!

Obtaining the license helped our marriage. Marriage is composed of so many complex factors, many of them abstract, that it sounds almost silly to say a marital relationship changed when the husband got a driver's license. Certainly someone counseling prospective spouses would not tell them a prime determinant of the success of their marriage was whether one or both of them had a driver's license. Yet in our case it meant a lot. It removed a barrier that had existed throughout most of our marriage — a barrier most important in my employment efforts, but having many other aspects.

Heather told her mother that she had a good time going to the store with her dad driving the car. Three or four times right after I got the license, she greeted me by smiling and saying: "Hello, Driver." I felt that I could relieve Silvia of some of the chauffering she had been doing of Heather and me, and of some of the errands she had run for the three of us. In a society that considers the auto a normal way of life, I felt like a more normal husband. No longer feeling "different" because I was the man without a license, I did not feel so "different" because I was the husband with a black wife. Most important, I no longer felt I was a slave to a master who could drive — no longer a slave to a black master who could drive.

The continuing decline in the economy in late December, 1974, made job hunting difficult, with or without a car. Early in January, however, I got a temporary accounting job which I could not have obtained without auto transportation. Then I spent two months earning just more than the minimum wage by doing income tax returns. Finally, about April 1, I became permanently employed, first with a subsidiary of a national firm and then with Dade County.

At home, several changes had taken place. We ate supper together a little more than we had in the past, and usually started with a prayer — something I had long recommended, but to which I thought Silvia was indifferent. I thought part of the reason was that she believed blacks had spent too much time praying and not enough time learning how to put more bread on the table. Once we agreed to do it, however, all three of us said we benefited from it. I had also associated with her race her desire to read a scriptual passage together, a desire she began

161

expressing several years earlier but which failed to excite me. During late 1974 we began doing this occasionally and agreed it was helpful.

In February I remembered our wedding anniversary, a tenth anniversary just as happy as our ninth anniversary had been sad. I had learned that such occasions should be celebrated even though our idea of celebration was merely going out to dinner at a restaurant with an inexpensive floor show. I had also learned that my wife was not unlike most wives when it came to expecting a little present on such occasions. This didn't overshadow the obvious — our biggest present to each other was living with each other. And after ten years of marriage, one little aspect of living together finally became a little bit of a problem, rather than being the aspect of the marriage where there always was complete harmony. The aspect was sex.

She wanted more than did I. I joked about the stereotype of blacks being more sexually aggressive than whites. I remembered the two times she told me that black men had invited her to their rooms at conferences. Of course I knew she would not accept such invitations, and of course I knew such things went on at all sorts of conferences and business meetings, but sometimes I pushed aside these facts and thought of her as one of "those blacks" preoccupied with sex. But despite these moments of my irrationality, this problem was not a racial one. Besides that, it was not much of a one at all: it no longer existed once I stopped spending my nights writing this book.

I suggested we attend a dance Saturday night, May 12, at the Unitarian Church to celebrate our year of having lived with each other. Unlike usual, Silvia was not too excited about going to a dance. Perhaps she was thinking of my lack of enthusiasm for and inability at dancing. I said that this was a special occasion and that we should honor the event. We went. The dance music was mediocre as far as Silvia was concerned. I fell asleep. But the occasion was happy. A renewal had occured during the preceding twelve months. We were delighted by that. We were happy that the renewal seemed permanent. We knew that renewal was going to last for months and years. Whether it would last forever we could not know, for we were living in the

162

world of the present. We wondered just a little bit about how our marriage would look from a viewpoint beyond the world, a viewpoint unlimited by the world's time, unrestricted by man's perspective, removed from human emotion, divorced from worldly prejudices.

CHAPTER X

Far And Near

The time is definite: now, today. The place is not so definite. It is far enough from the earth to be removed from the emotions and actions of the earth, so close as to make it possible to bring those emotions and actions sharply into focus. The area looks something like a room, but it is not quite like a room. Inside the area stands something that is not a table but looks much like a table. At the table sits someone who is not a human being, yet very much like one. He wears what looks like a business suit, has medium length hair with slight sideburns, and wears no tie. The only identification on the wall is a small certificate saying CONSULTANT, with small letters at the bottom reading "Licensed by Supreme Power."

With Consultant is someone — two people — two people who could be any two people happening to be of the opposite sex, the opposite race, and the same marriage. These two people happen to be named Pat and Silvia Huber. As they sit selfconsciously in two black chairs with white trim, Consultant speaks:

As I believed I explained in my brief earlier meetings with you, I have been commissioned by my employer, the Supreme Power, to examine several hundred interracial marriages during the last several years and report to him my findings. He recognizes the increasing importance of this matter and has asked myself and several colleagues to provide him with the data that will enable him to determine the ultimate truth about this question. I thank you for your cooperation in this study. Please speak frankly and openly to me. Nothing you say here can be held against you, either in your present life or in your afterlife. As you know, our location is very close to the real world, so close as to understand its day to day operations; but it is slightly removed from the real world, and that enables you and others to speak with more candor and from a point of greater perspective than you otherwise would be able to speak. I should like to start out by asking each of you if you believe your being different colors was important or unimportant in your married life?

164

MRS. HUBER: I'd say it was not important most of the time, even though it was important sometimes. During our first six or seven years of marriage, it did not seem important. About the only time it seemed important was when it gave us a feeling of togetherness or uniqueness, like being the only biracial couple in a neighborhood, or at a party, or in a church, or anywhere else.

MR. HUBER: I agree basically with you. Certainly it did not bother us during those early years. And certainly we, particularly I, often had a feeling of happiness and importance because of being the unique couple. I can see now, however, that even though we considered ourselves to be uninfluenced by our biracialness, we actually were influenced by it. This influence just didn't come to the surface until the 1970's.

MRS. HUBER: You think so? I don't agree with you on that. I didn't feel any influence and you didn't tell me you were influenced. When were you influenced?

MR. HUBER: I was influenced whenever there was a decision to be made about our lifestyle: I assumed you felt fortunate to have married a middle class white and so would not notice any economic restraints I put upon you, or upon us. Being married to you made me feel obliged to be more liberal and more pro-black than I otherwise might have been. You can see this by recalling some of the newspaper articles I wrote. I felt obliged to "show the other side" to white Americans. And when I was working for that trade publication, I remembered the working conditions you said your mother faced in the garment industry, and so I spent several days trying to write about this even though that was not the sort of thing the readers of a garment industry trade magazine want to read about.

CONSULTANT: What you are saying, then, is that even though having a black wife did not affect significantly your relationship to her during the 1960's, it did significantly affect you otherwise. Are you saying that this influence was primarily negative?

MR. HUBER: No. At the time I would have been very vigorous in answering no. I still say no, but now not quite so vigorously. I say no partly because I needed the influence in some ways.

It prodded me to do morally correct things which I would not otherwise have done. Sometimes it enabled me to approach race-related matters from a more intelligent viewpoint, or in a more skilled manner than would otherwise have been possible. And whereas sometimes being married to a black prodded me into saying or doing things that were desirable, other times it gave me peace of mind in doing nothing about a racial situation about which I should or I could do nothing. Instead of having a guilty conscience about not doing something or writing something to help a black, I had my wife's assurance that help was not needed or practical. That assurance meant much more than it would have had it come from a white wife.

CONSULTANT: You both have limited your comments to importance during the 1960's. How about those years in Miami?

MRS. HUBER: About that time our color difference became important. One reason was Heather. As she got beyond the crib stage, she became a constant reminder that her parents were not the same color.

MR. HUBER: No doubt about that. I believe the important thing was that we, like most parents, used our own childhood as our primary guide for raising our child. This emphasized to us the great difference between our childhoods, a difference we had not talked about extensively in earlier years.

CONSULTANT: In your book, Mr. Huber — by the way I did read it — I seemed to detect a recurring theme that when things were going well in your marital life, they were made just a little bit better by your biracialness, and when things were going badly they were made a little bit worse by your biracialness. Is this partly why you attach more importance to your biracialness during your Miami years?

MR. HUBER: Very definitely. Due to a combination of factors, many of which were of my own making and most of which were unrelated to race, I was an unhappy person during most of my time in Miami. I would have been unhappy married to any person. Because I was frustrated by unemployment and a feeling of failure, I wanted somebody on whom to blame my failure. I chose Silvia.

166

MRS. HUBER: Why did you choose me?

MR. HUBER: I've asked myself that question and finally came up with this theory. It's similar to what I was going to say on that TV show in Miami on which we were supposed to appear. When anybody blames anybody for anything, he cannot attack the characteristics of that person identical to his own, for in doing that, he condemns himself as well as the other person. He must find characteristics to attack which are not similar to his. When your spouse is of a different color and culture, there are plenty of dissimilar characteristics, and so there are plenty of characteristics to attack. Once you start attacking the characteristics of that person of a different color, pretty soon it becomes easy just to attack his or her color.

CONSULTANT: I have taken notes on your theory and am going to report it to my boss. The one question I would raise is how you regard yourself as so dissimilar to this woman with whom you have lived happily, just because she has a different color and culture? What happened to all your similarities?

MRS. HUBER: I was wondering the same thing.

MR. HUBER: It's hard to explain. It's not logical, but I was depressed enough to be illogical. I wanted an excuse for my lack of success, and wife's race seemed to be the only one available. And there were a few facts and the speculation of others to back up my contention. One job I had lost during the 'sixties was the result of my being married to a black, Silvia and I agreed to that. I had always made it clear to myself, to her, and to others, that race was no factor in the other job situations. In the 1970's, however, I began reviewing this conclusion with the intention of making her the scapegoat for all of my employment problems. I contended, with some accuracy, that my aggressive reporting had always been influenced by my being married to a black. I pointed out, with some accuracy, that my work at Aristar was not made any easier by the negative remarks I heard about members of my wife's race.

CONSULTANT: For you, Mrs. Huber, was there anything besides Heather that seemed to make color a more important factor in your marriage during the 1970's.

MRS. HUBER: The racial environment in Miami. We had come to Miami after assurance from a lifelong resident, a friend of a friend, that Miami was progressive with regard to race. He was comparing it to the Old South, we found out later, not the country as a whole. This has shown me the importance of the geographical area in deciding whether a given interracial couple can have a successful marriage.

MR. HUBER: I agree strongly, even though I had no concern about coming to Miami. It is always dangerous to generalize, but here goes: I agree with those who say that in many ways there is more discrimination in the north than in the south. But discrimination in the south is more open. This blatant discrimination made us more conscious of our color difference, and it made our color difference a more important factor in our marriage if for no other reason than we were more conscious of it. I suspect that other biracial couples would also find that their color difference is more important in an area that is more color conscious. Just because they'd find the color difference more important, though, does not mean it would necessarily be a negative factor. Have you come to any conclusions about this, Consultant?

CONSULTANT: Most of the data I have shows that a couple's color difference is important in proportion to the prevailing color consciousness of the area. But as you have pointed out, the increased importance of the difference may be positive as well as negative. Silvia, were you more conscious of being a black when you lived in Miami than when you lived elsewhere?

MRS. HUBER: Yes. Not a lot, but to some extent. Actually when we were in the north, it so happened that much of the time we associated with people who were not particularly race conscious. This was not because they were northerners, but just due to the nature of the situation. I agree with Pat's explanation of this early in the book where he talks about race being no big factor to the college friends with whom we associated before marriage, no live issue in the almost all-white areas we lived in during most of the 1960's, and no oddity in the predominantly black ghetto of Fort Greene. In Miami the situation was dif-

168

ferent. We associated mostly with whtes, and many of them were from the mainstream of life and so were more race conscious than those from the academic world, social service agencies, and newspaper businesses we had known in the north.

CONSULTANT: You haven't answered my question as much as I would like for you to do. I understand that the nature of your friends and other acquaintances in Miami made you a little bit more conscious about being black. But was there anything else that made you feel more black than you had been earlier in life.

MRS. HUBER: I'd say the biggest thing was the nature of my work. Until Miami, the people with whom I worked were not particularly conscious of color, or at least didn't indicate it. And the jobs I had were not related to my being black. At the University of Miami, they were. In the personnel department, and even more so in the Affirmative Action Program, I was a black trying to serve the interests of blacks in their relationships to white administrators.

MR. HUBER: I agree. You could not help but be more conscious of being black.

CONSULTANT: You agree that Silvia's jobs at the university made her more conscious of her blackness, but what do you conclude from this? Are you suggesting your marriage would have been better, at least easier, if Silvia had stayed away from jobs closely related to racial matters? Are you telling other blacks and whites not to marry each other if either plans a career involving racial matters?

MRS. HUBER: No. That's not what we're saying. That's not what I am saying, anyway. I did not have to make a choice between my very self-fulfilling work and my husband. And even if we had gotten divorced, I would not have blamed it on my job.

MR. HUBER: I agree. Now looking at the whole thing from this broad perspective, from this room or whatever it is somewhat above the world, it is clear that your job brought out the blackness in you faster than it otherwise would have emerged; but a lot of it would have come out eventually anyway. I, like

169

most whites married to blacks, would have had to deal some-time with my mate's sense of blackness. Perhaps your job gave us the benefit of giving me an earlier look.

CONSULTANT: Are you saying that Silvia's career was no factor so far as the biracialness of your marriage was concerned?

MR. HUBER: Not at all! It was a big factor, and it still is! It is something we did not take into consideration enough before getting married. We needed to look at ourselves not merely as black wife and white husband, but as black wife doing such and such a kind of work, and white husband doing such and such a kind of work. Silvia's career did not completely change her attitude about members of the white race, but it influenced it. I was not taking this influence into consideration at the time I married her. Any white and black thinking about marriage needs to do what we did not do: think about how race will affect their marital relationship in employment situations they are likely to have in the future, not just in terms of their present jobs, or in terms of no jobs at all.

MRS. HUBER: This was taken into consideration by a couple we knew, a couple who was very serious about each other when they ate dinner in our apartment in early 1968. The girl was a friend of mine, a black; the fellow was white, was interested in politics, and was working on the staff of Senator Robert Kennedy. They later concluded that although their love for each other was genuine, a black wife would conflict with the man's career ambitions. Usually the potential conflict of the respective careers of a black and white is not so obvious, and unfortunately often is ignored until after they are married and the conflict emerges.

MR. HUBER: I think another way the atmosphere in Miami affected your image of yourself as a black, and, consequently, your relationship to me, was that you were less secure as a black in Miami than you had been anywhere else.

MRS. HUBER: That's not true! How come you say I was less secure?

MR. HUBER: You talked more frequently about injustices

170

whites committed against blacks. For the first time in our marriage you became critical of numerous blacks, both of the Uncle Toms who were looking out only for themselves, and also of those blacks who failed to make use of the opportunities they had. Remember the clerical worker at the University of Miami whom you criticized for being too interested in boyfriends to spend time earning the degree she was capable of obtaining? I think you were beginning to worry if blacks were really on the way up, as you once believed, and I think this made you assert yourself to me.

MRS. HUBER: Nonsense. Certainly I was concerned when blacks, when anybody for that matter, did not make use of the educational opportunities afforded them; but that didn't mean I was insecure. You are right in suggesting I didn't start calling people Uncle Tom until after we lived in Miami, but that's just because I had not run across very many before that. I was mad at such blacks, but that didn't make me lose confidence in blacks.

CONSULTANT: Obviously you disagree as to whether Silvia's self image, and hence your relationship to each other, was affected by the Miami racial environment. But in spite of your lack of agreement, it seems there is something you can agree upon in regards to this. Mrs. Huber, would you say that since your husband *thought* your insecurity as a black person increased, this created a problem between you, even though you are confident that you had no sense of insecurity?

MRS. HUBER: I guess I would have to say yes. At the time I didn't know he felt I was insecure and consequently trying to dominate the white to whom I was closest; but if he had that feeling, obviously it was a problem.

CONSULTANT: Transferring to a new environment, then, might seem to affect one's attitudes towards one's race or that of one's mate. Regardless of whether it actually does, one spouse's believing it has had an effect, creates a potential problem. You, like many couples with whom I have talked, aparently failed to examine with each other as thoroughly as necessary the attitude each of you had about whites and about

171

blacks, given a change in environment.

MRS. HUBER: We ignored the importance to our marital relationship of the importance one of us attached to race, compared to the significance the other one of us attached to it. We always knew we agreed about racial principles, but we failed to realize we also needed some appreciation of the racial consciousness our spouse had in regards to both blacks and whites.

MR. HUBER: Yes. And we forgot that just because we understood each other's attitudes in one environment, this did not mean that we were automatically going to understand them in a different situation.

CONSULTANT: Many interracial couples are particularly concerned about the welfare of their children. The Supreme Power is naturally concerned about this, and probably will deal with it in his statement of the ultimate truth about interracial marriage. Now you told me earlier that as your youngster got older, you became more conscious of your color difference; and this consciousness sometimes brought about negative results. Would you conclude that your youngster has brought you more grief and less happiness than would a youngster with parents of the same color?

MR. AND MRS. HUBER (*speaking together*): Not less happiness.

MRS. HUBER: We talked about some of the racial tension between us that was generated or at least symbolized by her; but in spite of the problems we have had because of being biracial parents, we have had just about as many joys which we would not have had if we had been the same color.

MR. HUBER: I agree basically, although I have felt more anguish from being a biracial parent than has Silvia. This is what I talk about in the eighth chapter of my book.

CONSULTANT: Why have you had more anguish than your wife?

MR. HUBER: Primarily because the child is more hers than mine, partly because the child is her gender, and partly because a biracial child, according to the books we've read, must out of

172

necessity have more identity with the black than with the white parent.

MRS. HUBER: I think that's a fair way to put it. Until we got in this place here today and could look at things with a little more insight than is available to human beings, I did not realize that you considered yourself less than half a parent. Now I can see why you do. I can't criticize you for it: I don't know how it could have been otherwise.

CONSULTANT: Forgetting a moment about the effect your biracial child had on your marital relationship, what effect has her biracialness had on her? Is it negative or positive?

MR. HUBER: Positive, I would say.

MRS. HUBER: She has enjoyed the "uniqueness" of being biracial. This is partly because she is very aggressive and hammy as well as intelligent. Obviously a soft-spoken bashful youngster would not get so much pleasure out of being different, and might be bothered by it. But one benefit Heather has gotten from being biracial that any biracial child probably receives is an ease in dealing with people of either of two races, rather than those of just one race.

CONSULTANT: Have there been any negative factors?

MR. HUBER: No great ones, as far as I can see.

MRS. HUBER: The problems have not been great, but more important than you realize. I don't know if it is because as a father you don't have as much concern as a mother about most things, racial or otherwise, or because as a white you don't understand the problem a biracial child has in deciding what color he is.

MR. HUBER: I remember my passing off your being upset when some kid called Heather a nigger when she was five or six. Although any non-white child faces the possibility of such an insult, I did not think it was anything to worry about. If I had been black, I could have better understood the impact of the insult.

CONSULTANT: That's an interesting point. Although the

biracial child faces no greater risk of racial insult than a black child, only one of his parents, the black one, can understand it fully, whereas the black child has two parents presumably in a position to understand.

(Mrs. Huber put her hand over her mouth, trying to hide a yawn as she relaxed while listening to the discussion of biracial children, a subject which had rarely bothered her or her husband, even during their separation from each other.)

CONSULTANT: Now I'd like to concentrate on your families and the effect your biracial marriage had on them. First let's talk about the woman's family.

MRS. HUBER: My relatives, particularly my mother, have never felt close to Pat. The biggest reason has not been the color difference, though, but the language barrier. And the next biggest barrier has not been color but rather economics.

MR. HUBER: I agree. That states the problem. Why we failed to overcome it is not so easy to answer.

CONSULTANT: You both seem to be avoiding the basic question. Did Pat's being white have a negative effect on his relationship with Silvia's family?

MRS. HUBER: I'd say no.

MR. HUBER: So would I. I didn't look down on them because they were black, and I don't think they looked down on me because I was white.

MRS. HUBER: You looked down on them not because they were black, but you looked down on them sometimes because they acted like most blacks in low income urban areas. You didn't scorn their color, but you scorned some aspects of their culture, which included their color.

MR. HUBER: That's the guts of it.

MRS. HUBER: You developed increasing respect for my sister, Benedicta, but that was as she went back to college, obtained her B.A. and then her masters while working and raising a family at the same time. You respected her not because she was

174

black, or in spite of her being black, but because she was acting in accordance with the "white middle class formula" — which is to work hard, study hard, and reap the benefits.

MR. HUBER: You put it well. One thing I'd like to say about your relationship to your own family: I don't think you feel quite as close to your mother as when you were married. For her, things are about what they were in 1965 as far as finances, culture, and environment are concerned. For you, they are very different. The difference would be about the same if you had married a black, but I wonder if maybe your family doesn't attribute some of this difference to your having married a man of a different race.

MRS. HUBER: I don't think that is so.

MR. HUBER: How about you? I sometimes feel you are bothered by getting further from your family and blame me for it.

MRS. HUBER: That's not correct. How could you say something like that?

MR. HUBER: You have told me recently, a lot more than you did at the time, that you felt a long ways away from everybody when we were living in Ohio.

CONSULTANT: Would you say, Mrs. Huber, that this concern about geographical separation from your family was similar to that any wife would have felt in the same situation? Or did you feel a little more separated because you were not only living several hundred miles from your family, but were in a predominately white, English-speaking area?

MRS. HUBER: I hadn't thought of that, but it is a good point. I'd agree that having a husband of a different race made it a little easier for me to feel separated from my family.

CONSULTANT: How about your family, Mr. Huber?

MR. HUBER: It made it a lot easier for me to feel separated from my family. I didn't notice this for years, because I wanted to be further away from them than I had been, not because of any friction but merely because it seemed desirable to emerge from my protected small-town childhood environment. I only came to realize how much further my black wife had made me feel from my family when in about 1970 I started wondering if I should have left the environment in the first place.

CONSULTANT: Did your distance from your parents cause friction between them and you, or between your wife and them?

MR. HUBER: No. Not friction. But I can't help but think that as my parents saw their son become less than he might have become, they could not help but relate this to the fact that he was also the son who had married the black woman. This is just supposition, because my parents were always very discreet about blaming any of my shortcomings on my wife or on her color. Now if I had obtained achievements equal to or greater than our expectations, this problem would not have existed. But after they had been very loving and very good parents, after they worked hard to stimulate their youngster intellectually and sent him through graduate school, only to see him end up on an unemployment line, they naturally wondered why. My dad said to me in 1965 or 1966 that he wondered why I was having employment problems since I had had no problems in high school. He said that it must have been something at Columbia, since I seemed to be very happy and successful in undergraduate school, academically, socially and otherwise. He was looking for an answer as to why his son turned out different than either he or his son expected. He made sure he said nothing about my wife, but it would have been impossible for him not to think about her during a time like that.

CONSULTANT: Mr. Huber, did you ever feel your parents rejected you or were at least angry because you married a black woman?

MR. HUBER: Definitely not. Concerned, yes, but never angry. And their concern was controlled and rational. It was not about what my interracial marriage would do to harm them, but rather about what problems it might cause me.

CONSULTANT: Did you expect them to be concerned?

MR. HUBER: No. Not really. That's an important point. They, particularly my father, were very openminded about other racial and ethnic groups and had spoken favorably of interracial couples. But when it involved their son, they saw problems. I would strongly urge all whites contemplating marriage to a black to realize that no matter how tolerant their parents might be of biracial marriage, it is a completely different thing to think about it in the abstract than it is to have their child actually engage in it.

CONSULTANT: Mrs. Huber, did being black affect your relationship to your husband's parents?

MRS. HUBER: I am not positive, but I do not think so. I never felt close to Pat's father, but that didn't seem to have anything to do with race. Pat assured me it did not. I have always felt close to his mother. I realize, and she realizes, that we live in two different worlds, different not only because of race, but because of geography, occupation, and other things. We never have let living in different worlds keep us from being close together.

CONSULTANT: In your particular biracial marriage, please tell me what one action or attitude you found most helpful to you that would not have been so important had you been the same color.

MR. HUBER: That's easy. Our relatively long courtship, and our use of that time to talk about our proposed marriage in great detail. I believe in long and thoughtful courtships for any couple, but it is much more important for a biracial couple — at least it was for us. We dealt with many potential problems in an abstract, rather intellectual manner that would have been difficult to deal with in the same manner once we were married. And a long courtship should not be difficult for a biracial couple: after all the prime purpose of courtship is supposedly to permit two people to get to know each other; and if they are different color there is that much more for them to find out about each other.

MRS. HUBER: Your talking about a long courtship reminds me

of your telling me something about a white girl you knew in New York who married a black.

MR. HUBER: Oh yes. In that case the couple seemed to have about the same assets you and I have, and the girl's family was supposedly unbiased; but they got married in a hurry. I think she was pregnant. Anyway, in the suddenness of the marriage, the white was having second thoughts about the marriage, and told me her family refused to accept the black. She was defending her biracial marriage to her parents in mid-1963 somewhat like I was, but she was getting married the next month, whereas in our case there were two years to think about the desirability of the marriage. Once Silvia and I were married, we were convinced it was the right decision because we had deliberated about it for so long. In the case of the other couple, they were divorced in about a year. I don't know the details, but certainly they faced many problems that should have been discussed before they were married.

CONSULTANT: What's your response to this question, Mrs. Huber?

MRS. HUBER: I agree strongly with what he said. I'd carry it further and say that our marriage, even more than a marriage between members of the same race, was helped by genuine and extensive communication between us after the marriage day, not just prior to it. As long as the communication was good, our marriage was good. When the communication declined in the early 1970's, so did our marriage.

MR. HUBER: No doubt about that. We talked to each other just as much during the 1970's about racial matters as we had earlier, but we talked more about what others were doing and less about our relationship to each other.

CONSULTANT *(leaning back in his chair):* Now comes *the* question. Are you glad you married each other?

MRS. HUBER: I'm glad I married Pat. I think he has given me a lot, in spite of some frustrations he has caused me.

MR. HUBER: My answer would be the same.

CONSULTANT: Would your marriage have been easier or more

difficult if you had been the same color?

MR. HUBER: I can't answer that question. I don't think anybody can answer it thoughtfully because you can't change merely a person's color and nothing else about him. I don't know if I would have been happier married to a white Silvia than to a black one, because it is hard to imagine what she would be like if she were white. Would her personality be the same? Would her aspirations be the. . .

MRS. HUBER *(interrupting)*: I think that gets right to the point. We each found out during our marriage that one's race is not something that involves just the color of the skin. Your and my skin colors, I bet anybody's skin color, affects almost every aspect of his life. This is what the potential biracial couple must take into consideration.

CONSULTANT: Based on your own experience, would you advise a black and a white to be married?

MRS. HUBER: I think that's too general a question.

MR. HUBER: We cannot answer that question.

CONSULTANT: Does this mean our conversation here, your whole book, is of no help to a couple contemplating biracial marriage?

MR. HUBER: It means exactly the opposite! Our purpose is not to advocate or to oppose biracial marriage for a single couple; and the reason for that is that marrying a person of the opposite color can have both positive and negative effects.

MRS. HUBER: We wanted to point out some of the good influences our biracialness has had on us, and some of the bad influences, too.

MR. HUBER: Each couple can look at both these good and bad influences biracialness has had on our marriage and then attempt to determine which of these factors would be applicable to their marriage and which would not. Without sounding too much like an accountant, I am saying the day is past when the effects of biracialness in marriage are all liabilities, nor can they be considered all assets. There are entries on both sides of the balance sheet. And there is probably no couple with a balance sheet identical to that of any other biracial couple.

CONSULTANT: Three years' research on this subject has given me ample evidence to show that the effects of biracial marriage are not, to use your terminology, all assets or all liabilities. And certainly among the hundreds of couples I have interviewed, each couple's balance sheet was different from all others.

Thank you for showing us your balance sheet. It is from examination of such material that the Supreme Power will write his final report, *The Ultimate Truth About Interracial Marriage*. And I am sure you will be interested to know that he has already decided that there is no ultimate truth concerning the desirability or non-desirability of interracial marriage. His report is expected to say there are many potential plus factors and many potential minus factors that can occur as a result of a couple's biracialness. To use your terminology, the liability accounts and asset accounts must be examined for each couple to determine whether their prospective marriage would end up in the red or black — ah, excuse the figure of speech. I should say that the totals on the balance sheet for each couple will determine whether their marriage will be a profit or loss.

The End